Successful Happiness

How to Find and Fulfill Your Passion-Driven Purpose

Dr. William G. Dickerson

This book is dedicated to my beautiful wife,
who has been my best friend,
my partner in our passion-driven purpose,
a wonderful mother to our boys, and
an incredibly supportive lamplighter to my crazy ambitions.
My life would be empty without her.

CONTENTS

INTRODUCTION

After three decades of practice in dentistry, after founding and selling a postgraduate educational center, after learning about life and business from the school of hard knocks, and after sparring with my colleagues about professional concepts, I gave my final lecture.

It was at the annual meeting of the International Association of Physiologic Aesthetics in Orlando. Let me explain. Physiologic dentistry has now gained a position as a wonderful treatment philosophy for eliminating a lifetime of pain caused by a pathologic bite. It's called TMD (temoporomandibular disorder) and along with it is OSA (obstructive sleep apnea). This disorder can cause headaches, including migraines, neck and back pain, ear issues, and many other related maladies of the head and neck.

Many of my colleagues may still disagree about TMD's effects, because they don't know what they don't know, but they have a hard time explaining the success we have had in eliminating pain for our patients. Because of my convictions about our treatments, I became a target of criticism from the status quo. This is unfortunate, because I hoped to refocus the industry on the science and logic of this treatment modality, not on me. So by no longer lecturing outside of my LVI campus, I was able to change that focus. (It worked, by the way.)

Over a thousand people were present at the meeting—the largest crowd in IAPA's history. My final lecture was scheduled from 8 a.m. to noon. Since I had never done the lecture before, I had no idea how long it would take.

Doctors brought their kids, spouses, and teams to hear me speak. After I finished—four hours later—the entire audience gave me a standing ovation and wouldn't sit down or stop until I walked off the stage. Grown men in the audience were crying. Several people came up to me and gave me hugs while sobbing. That's not bad feedback from a crowd eager to eat lunch, attend other lectures, or visit Magic Kingdom.

The response to this lecture was better than I ever imagined. For example, one guy who had been criticizing me all year, and who even had to be removed from our professional forum for being so negative, walked up to me and told me it was the greatest lecture he'd ever heard. That surprised me because he was one of the most critical people I'd ever met. If the lecture helped him, then my hope is that it made a difference in many other lives that day as well. I know it made a difference in mine.

Afterward, someone suggested that I should write a book based on this lecture. So here it is.

What Do I Know? I'm Just a Dentist

This book, written in hopes of changing your life, comes from forty-two years of my business experiences. I've learned many lessons over those years. I turned an average dental practice into a highly successful cosmetic and restorative practice. I know what you're thinking: What do dentists know about business? Actually, not much. Most dentists are business idiots because we get no business education in dental school. I tell anyone interested in being a dentist to major in business because a dental practice is, in fact, a small business. Service is more important than product in business, and communication is critical—something lacking in most professional offices.

But I also founded the Las Vegas Institute for Advanced Dental Studies (LVI)—the most prolific and successful postgraduate dental educational center in the world—while overcoming insurmountable obstacles along the way. As the owner, I've observed thousands of our alumni and their practices. I know what has worked and what hasn't.

In addition to what I've learned through LVI, I started a Facebook patient discussion group for those suffering with TMD and OSA. This Facebook group has helped hundreds if not thousands of patients find relief from pain when no other medical professional was able to help. But I've also gained valuable knowledge from these patients as well.

I also became a student of business and have read hundreds of business books and publications. My practice first started to grow when I did my business homework. As a result, almost everything in this book came from someone who wrote a book or article about business principles. I've incorporated some of these ideas with my own knowledge and experience about business, along with my inherited commonsense principles. I have compressed all of this into ten simple steps.

This book also has life lessons that go beyond being successful in business. Even if you're not involved in some way with a business, you can apply the lessons in this book to your home and personal life. The same principles apply in every arena.

One of the lessons I learned was that you don't need an MBA to be successful in business. In fact, based on what I've experienced in the last four decades, I think an MBA kind of ruins people. It sometimes takes away their commonsense, so they just apply book knowledge to everything instead of using their head. Sometimes life is not that complicated.

I sold LVI in 2005 to a venture capital firm for more money than I ever imagined. Then I bought it in 2013. Why? In my opinion, the people with MBAs who were running it were not knowledgeable about running a business like LVI. We don't sell widgets; we sell dreams, hope, and knowledge through education. It's hard to put a value on something as esoteric as that. How do you base a business plan on an unmeasurable product? I'm not sure they teach that in business school. Sure, these were smart guys; but I don't think they grasped what the business of LVI was about. The experience of watching LVI being run by people who didn't have my passion for it also taught me a lot about business.

In reality, this book is just based on my years of life experience. Well, what is experience?

> Experience is simply the name we give our mistakes.
> **—OSCAR WILDE,** playwright

And that's the truth. Many times I didn't achieve what I wanted, but the situation provided me with an experience to figure out a better way to do it. Every technique we teach at LVI was usually developed because something didn't work, and we had to find a better way to do it.

I became a proficient problem solver. As a result, many of the steps I write about can help you achieve success. This book provides you with the experience of others so that you don't have to make the same mistakes.

> Experience is the teacher of all things.
> **—JULIUS CAESAR,** Roman politician

Some of you may still be saying, "Well, what do you know? You're just a dentist." Fair enough. Let's set aside that I also run a multimillion-dollar postgraduate center. But as I said, every dentist who owns a practice runs a small business. Most are smart, but many dentists and physicians mistakenly think they are smart in business. Because they think they are so smart, they don't see their business incompetence. It's what I call intellectual arrogance! Most dentists have been successful in their practices because they are competing against other business idiots. They think they are in the product business, and they aren't; they are in the service business. (More on that concept in step 9 of this book.)

To strengthen what I share in this book, I'm going to use other people's wisdom to make my points. I'm going to throw in lots of important advice and quotes from famous people. Maybe you will listen to them if you won't listen to me.

> My task, which I am trying to achieve is,
> by the power of the written word, to make you hear,
> to make you feel—it is, before all, to make you see.
> **—JOSEPH CONRAD,** Polish-British writer

At the end of this book is a section listing all the relevant business books I read to prepare my final lecture. Some of those are reflected in this book. I recommend you read them and others that may not be included. For any omissions, I apologize.

KEYS TO SUCCESS

What Is Success?

Ask yourself these questions:

- Are you as successful as you want to be?

- What is preventing you from reaching your desired success?

- Have you concluded that success is not in your cards?

- Do you believe that you can have the life you want, or do you think that it belongs to other people—to privileged people, the lucky ones somewhere else in the world?

- Do you think that successful people sacrifice too much? Are you uncertain about having to work that hard or sacrifice that much to be successful?

The definition of success is different in everybody's mind. Is it more money? Is it more free time? Is it respect? Maybe professional satisfaction? Happiness?

Because success is different for everyone, it is it important for you to define your success. If you haven't defined success for yourself, then how will you know when you've achieve it?

One definition of success that I like was from Bessie Anderson Stanley in 1904.

He has achieved success
who has lived well,
laughed often, and loved much;

who has enjoyed the trust of
pure women,

the respect of intelligent men and
the love of little children;

who has filled his niche and accomplished his task;

who has left the world better than he found it
whether by an improved poppy,
a perfect poem or a rescued soul;

who has never lacked appreciation of Earth's beauty
or failed to express it;

who has always looked for the best in others and
given them the best he had;

whose life was an inspiration;
whose memory a benediction.

I just think that's a great definition of success. Not once did she mention money. She says that true success is about being fulfilled in life. It's that feeling of deep satisfaction that starts in your soul and radiates through your being. The end result is happiness and peace of mind. That's how I view success. And I sincerely wish that for you. If everyone in the world was happy and successful, we wouldn't have so much violence, hatred, and evil. Maybe there would never be another war. If mass murderers and shooters who have plagued society were happy and at peace with themselves, they wouldn't have committed those heinous crimes. So why would anyone not want everyone to be happy and at peace with themselves?

Most people see money as the ultimate sign of success. We often consider the richest people in the world to be the most successful.

> Don't judge each day by the harvest you reap
> but by the seeds that you plant.
> **—ROBERT LOUIS STEVENSON,** Scottish novelist

But the truth is, our salaries improve if we focus on planting seeds—serving people and our relationship to humankind. If we do the right thing and we do it for the right reason, with the intent of improving someone else's life, we will usually be rewarded financially. Therefore, you don't have to choose one or the other.

> Success isn't just about what you accomplish in your life;
> it's about what you inspire others to do.
> **—UNKNOWN**

There is nothing wrong with money. Money is a good thing. Most philanthropic or altruistic good deeds are done by the wealthy. If you hate rich people, then that's just jealousy, which I address in a later chapter. There is nothing wrong with being wealthy. They say money is the root of all evil, but I don't agree. It's not the rich who commit most crimes. In their search for wealth, most are honest. In fact, searching for wealth was not the goal of the wealthiest people.

I hope each of you becomes extremely rich. But wealth should not be the only measure of success. It's just a way to keep score.

> Success is not the key to happiness.
> Happiness is the key to success.
> If you love what you are doing, you will be successful.
> **—ALBERT SCHWEITZER,**
> French-German theologian, philosopher

Talent and Hard Work

Perhaps you know someone who is very talented but who is unsuccessful. Maybe that person is you! Why is talent not enough?

> Talent is cheaper than table salt.
> What separates the talented individual from
> the successful one is a lot of hard work.
> **—STEPHEN KING,** American author

The point is this: talent may be given, but you must earn success. The world is loaded with talented people who never achieve their dreams. Are you gifted or talented at something? What have you done about it? The old saying is, don't wait for your ship to come in; swim out to it!

> The only place you will find success before work
> is in the dictionary.
> **—ARTHUR BRISBANE,** newspaper editor

How hard are you willing to work to achieve your dream? You may have a dream, but are you willing to work hard to achieve it?

> Some people dream of success
> while others wake up and work.
> **—UNKNOWN**

If talent was enough, how come I know so many talented people who are not successful? How is that fair? How does someone less talented become more successful than someone who is extremely talented?

> Getting ahead in a difficult profession requires
> avid faith in yourself. That is why some people with mediocre talent,
> but with the inner drive, go much farther than people
> with vastly superior talent.
> **—SOPHIA LOREN,** actress and singer

For you basketball lovers out there, which basketball players in history does this work ethic apply to? One would be Larry Bird. Yes, he was talented, but he had nowhere near the ability of Michael Jordan or a Kobe Bryant. But the guy worked very hard at his dreams. He had great inner drive. This country boy who was not particularly fast was one of the best in basketball. But it wasn't his talent that got him there. Don't get me wrong, both Michael Jordan and Kobe Bryant worked really hard as well. But talent alone does not equal success.

> I've got a theory that if you give 100 percent all of the time, somehow things will work out in the end.
> **—LARRY BIRD,** professional basketball player

Here's the problem: You can have all the talent in the world, and you can know what you're doing, but all that might not lead to success. Are you smart and talented? Are you working in that area right now? Are you making poor choices? Do you have the right attitude? We'll discuss that in step 3.

> For success, attitude is equally as important as ability.
> **—WALTER SCOTT,** Scottish novelist and poet

Intelligence and Self-Esteem

Many people have low self-esteem. Are you one of them? Do you think you'll never be successful because you're not smart enough? Think you didn't get the good genes from your parents? Do you believe that others are smarter than you? Well, that may not be true, and, truthfully, it doesn't matter. According to the book *Whose Life Are You Living? Discovering the Wisdom to Walk in Freedom* by Chidi Jacob:

- More than 50 percent of all CEOs of Fortune 500 companies had C or C- averages.

- 65 percent of all US senators were in the bottom half of their class. (That's not surprising.)

- 75 percent of all presidents were in the bottom half.

- More than 50 percent of millionaire entrepreneurs never finished college.

I saw a photo of a luxury car with this vanity license plate: 2.7 GPA. Now that's funny, but according to the statistics above, it is probably more common than we think. Kids, if you're reading this, don't pay attention to that. Go to college. It gives you a more distinct advantage in life. And you grow as a person being on your own. Now, saying that, it may distort your view of life, but getting out in the real world will usually bring you back to reality.

The point is that everyone has a talent. Develop the talent you have, not the one you want. But ask yourself why you want that one. Most of the time it's because you think it will make you more money. But you might not have any chance of attaining your desired talent. Don't spend time trying to strengthen your weaknesses. Instead, make choices that will add value to your talent.

Perhaps your talent lies in areas that you think are silly or imprudent. Maybe you think there is no way you can be professionally successful with your talent. Or perhaps you think it's too risky to pursue.

Richard Edler in his book *If I Knew Then What I Know Now* said this: "Safe living generally makes for regrets later on. Don't let yourself be pressured into thinking that your dreams or your talents are prudent. They were never meant to be prudent. They were meant to bring joy and fulfillment in your life."

Perhaps you think that your talent lies in a field other than your current profession. But maybe you just need to refine and improve your talent so that you can advance in your career.

So there we have it. It leads to the ten steps up the ladder to success:

STEP 1   Find Your Passion-Driven Purpose

STEP 2   Create Your Vision

STEP 3   Adjust Your Attitude—It's Everything

STEP 4   Eliminate Jealousy

STEP 5   Control Irrational Fears that Prevent Success

STEP 6   Master Your Desire and the Drive to Succeed

STEP 7   Persevere

STEP 8   Be Teachable

STEP 9   Serve Others

STEP 10   Find Happiness—The Ultimate Success

Of the ten, happiness is the most important. I don't care how successful you think you are; if you're not enjoying that success, it's meaningless. So, let's get started with finding your passion-driven purpose. That's the first step toward happiness.

STEP ONE
Find Your Passion-Driven Purpose

I believe passion is the foundation of success. Have you ever heard that before? Maybe you think it's just a silly statement or a clever phrase someone made up to sound inspirational. But the question is whether it is true.

Michigan researchers, in four detailed studies of 794 executives, measured how much importance people placed on feeling passionate about their work. Almost 80 percent of those studied said they thought it was important to follow their passion. By contrast, only about 20 percent believed that passion was less important. These people felt passion could grow with time and experience. Either way, the research implies that it's important to love what you do for a living.

> Pleasure in the job puts perfection in the work.
> **—ARISTOTLE,** Greek philosopher and scientist

The only way you'll be great at what you do is to love what you do. The problem is most people don't prioritize life around their passion. Many think that following one's passion is imprudent. They believe it's best to stay in the family business, or find work that makes money. They give up what they really wanted to do because they don't think it would be profitable enough. So many people move to a location where they think business will be the best instead of living where they want to live. Life is too short not to live where you want to live.

I hear people complaining about the weather where they live and I ask them, then why do you live there? Or they choose a job or profession because they think there is more of a demand for it than what they really have a passion for doing. I'm sure many of you even had a guidance counselor tell you what field would be the best for you in order for you to be successful. But those counselors didn't know your heart. They didn't feel your passion.

In a fantastic study, Robert J. Kriegler and Louis Patler followed fifteen hundred people for twenty years. Now that's a committed research project. They divided them into two groups: Group A, which comprised 83 percent of the research pool, chose their occupations to make money. Group B, which comprised 17 percent of the group, chose their occupations to pursue something they loved—they would worry about money later.

Now, here's the interesting twist: of the fifteen hundred people, 101 became millionaires, or 6.7 percent. Guess which group they were in? Surprise! One hundred of the millionaires were from group B. Only one was from group A. About 40 percent of those who followed their passions became millionaires. That's an incredibly high rate!

This makes sense because when people choose a career path based on how lucrative they think it will be, they don't follow their hearts. They mistakenly believe that their passion won't lead to wealth.

A friend of mine (let's call him Brett) became a dentist, but he really wanted to be a writer. He never developed what he would call a very successful dental practice. He would say he's not very successful. He's a great dentist and he's made a good living, so he's successful, but nearly every dentist has the dream of building a top practice.

Brett went through many life-threatening obstacles along the way, which led him to finally write a book that he thought about for a decade. Writing was always in the back of his mind and something he always wanted to do, but he kept putting it off. Life got in the way.

Well, his book is now published. It's titled *Simplifying Life: Simple Steps for Finding Your Way (in a Complex World)*. It's a great book with valuable life messages. It's written in a humorous manner that's easy to read. Brett finally achieved his dream—he's a published author. His success led me to finally write this book. Thanks mate, for the inspiration. Love and gratitude!

Passion is the first step to achievement. Love what you do. The only way you can achieve anything significant is to want it, and passion is the key to make you really want it.

How many times have you set out to do something only to find that the drive wasn't there? How many New Year's resolutions have you made that you never kept? You gave up because you weren't passionate about it, so the drive wasn't there.

EXERCISE
List Three Things You Are Passionate About

What are you most passionate about? Without listing your family members, write down three things that you're passionate about. This is an important way of discovering how to change your life, so please do it.

Did you do it? Come on, just do it. If you did, proceed. If you didn't, I'm not going to let you read anymore until you do. Okay, I know I can't stop you, but please do this exercise.

EXERCISE
List Your Three Top Talents

What are your top talents? List your top three.

After you have done that, answer this big question. Do your top talents match with your passions? How many are the same?

Comparing your two lists is important because talent without passion is worthless. What carries people to the top is passion. Talent and passion need to be aligned.

Passion creates energy. It provides what I call the three Es of success:

• Excellence

• Enthusiasm

• Energy

Excellence is related to your talent, something you're good at doing. Enthusiasm and excitement pertain to your passion. Energy is necessary for success, because it is hard work to be successful.

If you think success is going to be easy, you're wrong. It's why this book contains the ten steps up the ladder to success, not down the ladder. There are easier choices, but the path to success is not going to be easy. In fact, there is no easy path. However, if you're passionate about what you are trying to accomplish, it won't seem like work, but rather a hobby. Sure, it will be time consuming, but it will be a labor of love.

Even if you are excellent, a lack of energy will prevent you from being successful. If you're not passionate (enthusiastic) about what you're doing, you won't have the energy. And you won't be passionate about what you're doing if you don't feel you're excellent, or at least striving for excellence. All three of those factors are tied together, so it's imperative to have all of them working.

My oldest son, Dylan, graduated from college with a degree in political science. But he had no interest in it. It wasn't his passion. As a result, he didn't do anything with that degree. So, he set off to see the world—with my approval and my encouragement. I told him to go find his passion.

He found it. He is now a marketing filmmaker for businesses. He does this while he travels the world to see life in other places, usually tropical paradises. He's experienced Thailand, Vietnam, Cambodia, Laos, Guatemala, Costa Rica, Columbia, Bolivia, and Cuba (at the time of this writing). He settles down in remote places for a while and uses his talents to pay his way and make a living. He's very talented at this and he loves it.

He formed his company and calls it DJD Creative Productions. I believe he's found his future. We'll see, but for sure he's found his passion.

Are you passionate about your job? Are you passionate about your life? Do you look forward to your work every day? Do you look forward to getting up in the morning? If not, follow your heart. Direct your life to concentrate on your passion.

- If it's painting, be the best painter you can be.
- If it's music, be the best musician you can be.
- If it's dentistry, be the best dentist you can be.
- If it's golfing, be the best golfer you can be.
- If it's photography, be the best photographer you can be.
- If it's writing, be the best writer you can be.

Whatever it is that makes you feel alive, direct your energy toward the goal of becoming the best you can be. Life is too short not to feel passionate about what you do every day. Now, if that is how you feel, fantastic. Congratulations! The next chapters will teach you how to turn that passion into success. But for those who are not passionate about life or profession, stop and think about this quote.

> I would rather die of passion than of boredom.
> **—VINCENT VAN GOGH**, artist

Let's say your career is not fun anymore. Why are you no longer passionate about your work? Can you become passionate? And how will that be done?

When I went into dentistry, I would have been in group A in the study I mentioned earlier. I did it because I liked working with my hands. I thought I could make good money doing it, and I liked the fact that dentistry would be a nine-to-five job. My dad was a lawyer and he would study cases with stacks of paper and books all night. I was not a fan of school and homework, and I didn't want to do that for the rest of my life.

When I first got out of dental school, I was excited about it. It was new and I was starting my adult life. But it didn't last. About five years later, I was burned out. If I could have done anything else, I would have quit being a dentist. But dentists are relatively one-dimensional characters. There's not a lot you can do with a dental degree other than be a dentist. It certainly wasn't my passion.

About that time, I went to hear a famous dentist, Dr. Omer Reed, who has been a life-long mentor of mine. It's important to have mentors. He made me realize that I didn't have to lack passion for my job. He changed my perception of how I should be treating people and my practice. He challenged me to change, and change I did. I made significant transformations in my practice in what he called "front-desklessness." I called it a patient-centered practice. I followed his guidelines for how a guest (patient) would be treated and cared for in our office. I didn't change any clinical procedures, just the service aspect of my practice. This changed my life and started the ripple effect from which LVI emerged. Love and gratitude, Omer!

At about the same time, a local lab sent me a voucher to attend a seminar. If I attended, they would provide a free tooth-colored restoration, which is what the seminar was about. The material was called Concept. It replaced the ugly silver-mercury fillings that most dentists were placing at the time. I said I would go, but like most dentists, I skipped the seminar. Why? Because dentistry wasn't my passion. Why would I spend time away from my life to spend more time on work? Lack of passion is the reason that 80 percent of dentists don't go to continuing education programs beyond what they need to keep their licenses. It's a shame that they are forced to learn instead of having a thirst for knowledge.

The lab that was putting on the seminar called me and told me they would still provide a free restoration if I wanted to try it on one of my patients. So I agreed to the offer. The restoration was beautiful. I then started learning all I could about adhesive dentistry, which led me into porcelain veneers and other methods for improving smiles. Because I was doing more Concept restorations than almost anyone in the country at the time, the local lab asked me to do an evening lecture on it for a few local dentists. Thirty showed up. It seemed I was a natural at it.

I then fell into cosmetic dentistry, which is about making people happy and changing their lives. All of a sudden, dentistry became my passion. I started lecturing around the country about it, which eventually led to LVI. And with the constant evolution of LVI, I ventured into training thousands of dentists to treat TMD, and helped many patients who suffer from TMD, people who have suffered their entire lives with pain that no other health provider could eliminate.

It's so sad that many people are suffering and don't know there is help available. But the condition has to be treated physiologically, and most dentists are not trained in that. Now I'm passionate about that aspect of dentistry. This is truly my passion-driven purpose.

My wife, Heidi, is also a dentist. We work on TMD training and treatment almost every waking hour. So what I was trying to avoid by going into dentistry—the nighttime work—became a normal part of my life. But it doesn't seem like work. We love what we do, so the work is something we want to do, not something we have to do. We feel we are making a difference in the lives of many people.

> We all want to help one another.
> Human beings are like that. We want to live by
> each other's happiness, not by each other's misery.
> **—CHARLIE CHAPLIN,** silent film actor

I hope my story helps you realize that your passion is right in front of you, even if you can't see it. I went from hating what I did for a living to loving it. Many dentists who studied at LVI now love what they do for a living. Some older dentists tell me that they no longer want to retire. They found their passion right under their noses. That is the biggest compliment anyone can give me. It's not about how much money they are making.

Sometimes your passion-driven purpose is right in front of you. Maybe it's something you tried to avoid for various reasons. Maybe you will discover that a career path isn't what you thought it would be. For example, my daughter, Kimberlee, never wanted to follow in her dad's footsteps. She didn't want to be a dentist. So she got a marketing degree. She came to work for me at LVI in our marketing department and got to be around all the dentists who were happy and excited to be at LVI.

One day while working on our website, she needed to gather testimonials from doctors about how LVI had helped them love their work. She also collected testimonials from patients whose lives had been changed by the treatment provided by an LVI doctor. She realized at that moment that she wanted to feel about her job like the doctors she interviewed. Marketing was not her passion. She decided to go to dental school. She took her required science classes while continuing to work for us.

To make a long story short, today Kimberlee is an amazing dentist in San Francisco who practices with her husband. She loves what she does for a living. Her passion-driven purpose was right in front of her the whole time, but she didn't see it.

Maybe you once had passion, but you failed to do something with it and became discouraged. Failure puts out the fire of passion in many. Well, you can't let failure stop you from your mission. Everyone has failures; that's no reason to quit. I will talk about perseverance in step 7.

> Success consists of going from failure to failure
> without loss of enthusiasm.
> **—WINSTON CHURCHILL,** British prime minister

Talent is your strength. And passion—does it make you feel alive? Do you feel your passion-driven purpose? Passion increases willpower, which helps you work hard. You're less likely to quit if you have passion for what you're doing.

What do you care about? What do you laugh about? What do you dream about? Answer those questions to discover what your passion is. Someone once asked Ghandi, "Mr. Gandhi, you have been working fifteen hours a day for fifty years. Don't you think you should take a vacation?" Gandhi smiled and replied, "I am always on vacation."

Now I want you to list the three things that you spend the most time on.

EXERCISE

List Three Things You Spend the Most Time On

Let's compare those responses with your passion list. Do they match? Do any of them match? If they do, then congratulations! You've completed the first step toward achieving your dreams. If not, then let's think about how you can better align your passions with your time.

> It is the greatest shot of adrenaline
> to be doing what you've wanted to do so badly.
> You almost feel like you could fly without the plane.
> **—CHARLES LINDBERGH,** American hero

Or perhaps you have given up on your dream. You're convinced it's not in the cards for you. That hope of achieving your dream is gone.

> The tragedy of life is what dies inside a man while he lives.
> **—ALBERT SCHWEITZER,** French-German theologian

Sadly, too many people feel those losses. They have given up hope. Without passion, a part of us is dead. Passion is the foundation for excellence. Passion is the key to success. And passion is the foundation of life. It's imperative that you find your passion or, if you can, become passionate about what you do. It's possible. Look at me and the thousands of dentists who have been through LVI!

I love a movie called *Serendipity*. It's a chick flick, and I love chick flicks. I guess I'm a romantic at heart. In this guy-meets-girl movie, the girl writes her phone number in a book. The guy must find the book. He searches for years. But in the meantime, he becomes engaged to another woman.

To make a long movie short, he realizes that he doesn't have the passion for his fiancé. He has a lingering doubt about the girl he met one night and can't find. So he calls off the wedding. He asks his friend if he did the right thing. His friend, who writes obituaries for a living, said this: "You know, the Greeks didn't write obituaries. They only asked one question after a man dies: 'Did he have passion?'"

What would they say about you when you die, if they asked that question? Did you have passion? I hope they say that about me when I die.

So instead of spending time on things that are not your passion, try and spend more time on those that are your passion. Here is a way you can check to see how you're doing.

EXERCISE
Stop Now and Write This Down

I know you're getting tired of making lists. But this is important. Make the following lists.

- Three things that you should stop doing because they are not your passion.
- Three things you should keep doing because you are passionate about them.
- Three things you should start doing because they may be your passion.

Protecting Your Passion

Now, maybe you had passion and you lost it. As I mentioned earlier, that's not uncommon. So let's talk about protecting that passion. You need to feed your fire of passion. If you don't, the fire will go out. Not everyone in your life will help you do that. There are many reasons why people might not help you, but generally they are miserable, and misery loves company. I will address negativity in step 3.

So let's talk about protecting the passion you have, or had. It's natural for a fire to go out. It's natural for your passion to fade. It happens all the time. To keep the fire of passion hot, you need to defend it against those who want to extinguish it. Therefore, hang with lamplighters not candle snuffers.

Lamplighters will go out of the way to help you keep your fire lit. The candle snuffers will put out the flame of passion that burns within you.

How do you know if someone is a candle snuffer? Let me give you some candle snuffer language so you can identify one (and run the other way). They say things such as:

- That's not practical.

- We tried that before and it didn't work.

- We've never done that before.

- Yeah, but.

- If it ain't broke, don't fix it.

- It'll never work.

- That's not the way we do things.

- You're not smart enough, you're not talented enough, you're not good enough, you're not tall enough, you're not skinny enough, you're not pretty enough.

- You're getting too big for your britches.

- And who do you think you are?

That's all candle snuffer language. Do you know people like that? Avoid them. Candle snuffers focus on what's wrong rather than on what's right. They are the glass-is-half-empty types. They believe "every silver lining has a cloud." They resist change and they spread the negativity virus, which we'll also discuss later.

> Keep away from people
> who try and belittle your ambitions.
> **—MARK TWAIN,** American humorist

Negativity is like a computer virus that will destroy everybody in your office or family. It will crash the system. Candle snuffers can easily make a positive person negative. So keep your distance from these kinds of people, if you can't change them, which is hard to do.

> I will not let anyone walk
> through my mind with their dirty feet.
> **—GANDHI**

The movie *Pursuit of Happiness* is a true story about a father (played by Will Smith) who was homeless. Everybody had always told him that he couldn't do this, or he couldn't do that. As the man's son is shooting baskets, the son mentions he wants to be a professional basketball player. But the father conveys to his son that he is spending too much time playing basketball. He tells him he won't be any good at it because he (the dad) is not any good at it and that he doesn't want him wasting time on something that he won't succeed in. He tells him that he'll be good in other things, but not basketball.

The dad sees the kid is dejected as he throws the ball at the fence. It's obvious the kid is upset that his passion has been crushed.

Dad: (pausing and thinking about what he just did to his son) Okay? All right, go ahead. Hey, don't ever let somebody tell you you can't do something. Not even me, all right?

Son: All right.

Dad: (with much emotion) You got a dream, you got to protect it! People who can't do something themselves, they want to tell you, you can't do it! You want something, go get it! Period!

It was an emotional scene. Fortunately the dad saw he was being a candle snuffer, not a lamplighter.

The father (Smith) was trying to achieve his own dream to become a successful stockbroker, but people kept telling him he couldn't do it, that it was just too hard. Nevertheless, he succeeded in achieving his dream. It took hard work. He even goes through a time of selling sewing machines door to door. But he became rich by getting his foot in the door and persevering.

Watch the movie because it's a lesson to everyone who wants to achieve their dreams. I just spoiled it for you, but it's still worth watching. It is one of my favorite movies of all time.

Who are lamplighters? Lamplighters see the potential that you can be. They encourage your passion. They help you reach your dreams. They give constructive help, not phony encouragement. You can usually tell when it's phony. Hang with them as much as you can. Befriend people who see you as more than you currently are and who push you to excel.

At LVI, we look at the raw talent that comes through our doors. We know that people can be successful, regardless of whether they think they can or not. My passion-filled purpose is to change the world by changing the lives of as many people as I can. That positivity has become infectious. The alumni are quick to help out another LVI dentist. They encourage each other on our professional forum. The jealousy and competitiveness that is so prevalent in our profession is not common among LVI dentists. It's incredibly rewarding for me to see, and I'm very proud of this special group.

Make a list of people who try to snuff out the fire of your passion. This will be hard as some may be close to you. But it's important that you avoid them. If it's your spouse, get counseling. This is unfortunately more prevalent than you may think.

I had someone close to me in the past who would say, "Why are you working so hard on your lectures? Who's going to come to listen to you?" When I wrote my first dental business books, she would say, "Why are you writing a book? Who's going to read it?" In the many years I knew this person, she never said she was proud of me, never encouraged me to excel, never was a lamplighter in my life.

EXERCISE
Make a List of Candle Snuffers in Your Life
Try and avoid spending time with these people. It's not healthy for you.

EXERCISE
Make a List of Lamplighters in Your Life
Try to spend more time with the lamplighters. In fact, write them a thank you note. Give them love and gratitude.

Expressing love and gratitude to lamplighters in your life is important. The two greatest words in the English language are love and gratitude. Maybe you've heard about the book *The Hidden Messages in Water*. The Japanese researcher Masaru Emoto did an experiment. He took water from different areas of the world, and he put messages on the bottles of water. Sometimes these were written messages, and sometimes he had little kids say things to these bottles of water every day. Some of it was negative stuff and some of it was positive stuff. The negative stuff was like, "You make me sick." And he would freeze the water using a very sensitive technique. After freezing the water, he would be able to slice it and could look at the crystals that formed.

On the bottles of water that received the negative messages—"You make me sick," "You fool," "I hate you," "You're ugly"—the frozen water didn't form crystals or it formed misshapen crystals. But when the children said, "You're beautiful," he could see the beautiful crystals that formed. But the most beautiful crystals were formed from water receiving the messages of love and gratitude. When they put love and gratitude messages on the bottles or they said love and gratitude to the water, the most beautiful crystals were formed.

Think of this: You're 98 percent water. You need love and gratitude.

You may say that's a silly study, or not believe it. I get that. But the concept and message of the study is valid. Google it to see photos of the crystals. Life is better when you have love and gratitude in your life. Just say it now: love and gratitude. Use these words to be a lamplighter for other people.

Love and Gratitude

Doesn't it make you feel good just to say those words? I want you to close your eyes and think of a person whom you are grateful for having in your life and whom you love. It doesn't have to be a romantic love, just someone you love, and say those words as if you were saying it to their face. Now, think for a minute, didn't that make you feel good?

Every time I talk to my kids, I tell them I love them. They tell me they love me back. Sometimes they say it first. It has become a habit now. It's nice to hear a grown man (two of my boys are adults now) say to his dad, "I love you." My daughter and I say it every time we are about to get off a call. It's the same thing with my wonderful son-in-law. My wife and I say it to each other all the time.

So here's the truth: It was not easy for me to say that when I was younger. I had a hard time expressing love. I don't think as a young man I ever said it to my parents. The other day I took my ninety-five-year-old dad to lunch after getting him hearing aids. I told him I loved him and he said it back. It felt good. Truth is I never remember my dad saying it to me while I was growing up, so perhaps I was emulating the male role model in my life. I knew he loved me and he was a wonderful father. So perhaps it was my impression of what a man was supposed to be like, not expressing emotion or assuming that people knew you loved them.

If you feel uncomfortable with this, I get it. I was there. I think for whatever reason it's harder for males. Stupid macho thing gets in the way. But you can change. For you men reading this, be the role model for your own children and free them of the inability to express love and gratitude. It will make them loving and happy adults. Love and gratitude is the key to being happy. It's impossible to not be happy if you have love and gratitude in your heart. I now tell my male friends that I love them.

EXERCISE
Send Message or Call Now

Think of three to five people in your life who have inspired you or have been a lamplighter for you. Send them an email or private message them or call them and write or say, "I just wanted to say love and gratitude to you for being in my life." I know this might be hard for you, again, especially you men reading this. But once you get in the habit of saying it, it becomes easy. By doing this, you can make someone feel great for at least a day. It will be easier for you to text or email, but eventually work your way up to saying it face-to-face. Yes, it may even be uncomfortable for them, but you'll feel better and so will they.

Did you do it? If not, please, I am begging you to do this. Three to five people is all. If you did, didn't it make you feel good? Did they respond back yet? If they did, did you see how it made you feel? Then imagine that they felt the same way when they received your message. If they don't respond, it doesn't matter. You did your part and should feel good about it. Perhaps they were busy, or didn't know what to say because they haven't read this book. It doesn't matter. I promise you that you made them happy. And that's a good thing.

You see, we all need lamplighters in our life, and I'm fortunate to have lots of them. In fact, I'm married to one of the best. Going from a marriage where there was no love and gratitude to one where we certainly feel it every day and express it often makes a huge difference. In every card we give each other, in every discussion we have, in moments of sharing and closeness, we express love and gratitude. Maybe it's because we both came from unhappy marriages that it makes us appreciate each other that much more.

Do you feel love and gratitude about your significant other? Understand that if you have that, I think it's rare. I don't believe there are that many marriages that do. If you don't have it, do you know why? Can you find that love and gratitude? Have you even tried? If not, and I am reluctant to say this because people have religious constraints, but you need to be happy. In my opinion, no one should have to stay in an unhappy marriage. There is nothing more important than personal happiness. More on that in step 10.

Before I gave my final lecture, I received a book from a friend I'll call Laurie. It's the book by Randy Pausch, *The Last Lecture*. She was giving it to me to inspire me since I was about to give my last lecture outside of LVI. I stayed retired for eight years after that lecture and then started to do selective road lectures again because my kids were grown and independent. But the words she wrote inside were more important to me than the book.

She wrote: "Bill, maybe they will make yours into a book someday."

See? She gave me encouragement. She was lighting my fire. Look, that's what I'm doing now, making my last lecture into a book.

Then she wrote: "You have always been an inspiration to me. Thanks for changing my life."

She expressed gratitude while being a lamplighter. She's one of my favorite lamplighters. Why don't you become someone's favorite lamplighter? Love and gratitude, Laurie!

Before my final lecture, I also received another book titled *Speeches that Changed the World* from another friend I'll call Anne-Maree. She gave it to me when I arrived at the hotel to give my talk. Her message inside said: "No pressure, Bill. You have already changed the world more than you will ever know."

She is and has been an important lamplighter in my life. Love and gratitude, Anne-Maree! Why not make it your goal to become an important lamplighter in someone's life.

I also got a card when I arrived to speak from a friend named Joe. It said, "I believe in mind over matter. I believe in the human spirit to prevail. I believe in miracles and blessings both great and small. I believe in possibilities. I believe that hurdles in life are meant to be jumped over, not as something to stop us. I believe in you. Love you, man." Love and gratitude, Joe!

Love and gratitude encouraged me. My lamplighters were all lighting my fire before my talk. We all need our fire or passion protected and stoked so it stays lit. We all need to give love and gratitude as well to be happy. So make it a habit of yours. Every day, tell someone: love and gratitude.

How do you develop love and gratitude in your children? My wife and I tried to do that with our kids as they grew up. At dinner, we copied an idea that we had seen in the movie called *One Fine Day*. We would ask our kids to tell us about their "high" and their "low" of the day. And sometimes they had trouble coming up with the low, which was a good sign.

If we had somebody over for dinner, a visitor from out of town, for example, my kids would say, "My high today was that [blank] gets to be here at dinner with us." Or they'd say, "My high today was when Daddy picked me up from school." That was always nice to hear. I picked them up every day, so I think they just wanted to make me happy. But they were expressing love and gratitude. Try that with your kids, it's fun and will get you talking. They will have to put the phones down to be involved.

So express gratitude often. That will help you be a lamplighter for other people. Doing so will help them pursue their passions.

EXERCISE

Start Your Highs and Lows Tonight at Dinner

Wake up each day thinking about what you have to be grateful for and for all the love in your life. Think about someone you're going to say it to that day when you first wake up. When you start to get down or upset, just say love and gratitude over and over. Make yourself think about everything in your life that you do have to be grateful for.

The Importance of Relationships to Fueling Your Passion-Filled Purpose

Your relationships are critical to finding and pursuing your passion-driven purpose. If you think about it, most sorrows can be traced to bad relationships and most joys to good ones. Has a recent relationship drained you of enthusiasm, passion, and energy? All relationships require energy, even the good ones. I give my inner circle of friends everything I've got. And many give me everything they have.

One friend in particular goes out of his way to be a friend. He's generous and cares about Heidi and me with no hidden agenda. Let's call him Chong. He calls me with ideas to help the business even though there is nothing in it for him. He's a special lamplighter in our lives. It's obvious he cares about us. Love and gratitude, Chong!

> The glory of friendship is not in the outstretched hand,
> nor the kindly smile nor the joy of companionship;
> it is in the spiritual inspiration that comes to one
> when he discovers that someone else believes in him
> and is willing to trust him.
> **—RALPH WALDO EMERSON,**
> American essayist, lecturer, philosopher, and poet

I assume everybody knows who Helen Keller is. If you don't, she was born blind and deaf. And yet, she achieved incredible success as an author and learned to talk. How could she learn to talk without hearing the speech to emulate? She was amazing. Her mother was her lamplighter. She summed up relationships with the following statement:

> My friends have made the story of my life.
> In a thousand ways, they have turned my limitations
> into beautiful privileges and enabled me to walk
> serene and happy in the shadow cast by my deprivation.
> —**HELEN KELLER,** American author, political activist, and lecturer

Good friends are not phonies. They don't say, "Oh, yeah, sure, you can do it, jump." An old saying goes like this:

> In prosperity, our friends know us.
> In adversity, we know our friends.
> —**JOHN CHURTON COLLINS,** British literary critic

Boy, do I know that. Perhaps you've been betrayed, too. Many people pretended to be a friend to get something from me, or maybe for me to make them "famous." Running an educational institute, I had the position to put others on the stage, to give them an audience and the recognition they craved. I gave some of them my own presentations to use during their talks. These people would use me to build up their names and then compete against me and LVI. I'm sure you all know people like that.

Loyalty is a character trait that seemed to die with the Greatest Generation. We now live in a "me" society where others will step on people or betray them to get ahead. But life doesn't usually reward evil. I don't believe any of these people have achieved true success. I consider myself to be fiercely loyal and find disloyalty one of the most disgusting traits a person can have. I often wonder how people like that can sleep at night.

If your current friends aren't real friends, then make new ones.

So what is a true friend?

A true friend knows your weaknesses
but shows you your strengths, feels your fears
but fortifies your faith, sees your anxieties
but frees your spirit, recognizes your disabilities
but emphasizes your possibilities.
—WILLIAM ALLEN WARD, American writer

What type of people do you want in your life? Who will help you pursue your passion? Here is my list of qualities in a good friend.

Family, of course, unless they drain you of your energy. If they are a negative force, you don't have to spend time with them just because they're family. Some of you probably suffer with that situation. It's more common than you think. I know I did. Family can betray you just like so-called friends can.

Fun. When you talk about the best times in your life, it's always around fun. Laughter is the best medicine for life. When you laugh, you release endorphins that make you feel good. Do you take life so seriously that you aren't enjoying it? Do you not laugh at jokes? Do you think you need to be serious to be taken seriously? If you are not enjoying life, then do something about it. We will talk about the importance of happiness in the last chapter, but being around fun people will help you achieve that. Laugh daily, and out loud. This is your one shot, try to enjoy every minute. One of the most important traits someone can have is a good sense of humor.

Intelligent people, because they are great conversationalists. I think the reason my wife and I get along so well is because we are intellectual equals. I know this sounds bad, but I don't do stupid. It's just frustrating for me to have to deal with stupidity. But I love talking to intelligent people because I find them interesting and informative.

Those with a **thirst for knowledge** are interesting because they are interested. I love being around people who have a thirst for knowledge. They ask questions because they are interested. They are people who will grow along with you.

Motivators encourage you and give you confidence. I'm not talking about phonies who pretend to give you confidence. I mean people who say, "Hey, Bill, you should try this. You'd be good at it and love it." Or they encourage you to do something, like Brett encouraged me to write this book.

Successful people, because they have great stories that I can learn from. Successful people have usually achieved their passion in life. I find them interesting, and we can all learn from their successes.

Trustworthy people. With what I've been through in life, finding someone I can truly trust is critical. There are few people whom I can say that about. Certainly, my wife is someone I trust. She is the love of my life as well. We are together twenty-four hours a day on most days. We share the same office. She is not only my life partner, but my business partner, and I trust her. I like being around people I can trust. I know I can be honest with them because I know they won't turn my honesty against me some day.

Happy, positive people are infectious. I'm hoping this book is infectious. But I like happy people. You like being around people who are happy and positive, don't you? You hate going to the DMV because everyone is grumpy and hates their job. You like going into businesses where people seem to love what they do. One of the reasons that Starbucks has been successful is that it's usually a fun environment where people behind the counter are nice and happy. They know how to hire the "whos" not the "whats." More on that later.

Unfortunately, many who read this book will go home to a life with miserable, pathetic, and unhappy people who drain their energy. That can affect the drive towards your passion filled purpose. It's essential for you to vigorously protect your passion. Why? Because, again, it's natural for the fire to go out. So hang with lamplighters, avoid candle snuffers. Don't let negative people piss on your parade.

What's Your Passion-Driven Purpose?

Success through a passion-driven purpose is critical. Do you believe in your mission? Will people say life is better because of your mission? If not, it may not be worth doing.

> The purpose of life is a life of purpose.
> **—RALPH WALDO EMERSON,**
> American essayist, lecturer, philosopher and poet

> "Without meaningful work, life stinks."
> **—AL KALTMAN,** writer

I often wonder about that. How does someone who does nothing productive feel about life? A narcissistic person who spends days doing things for his or her own vanity needs and desires will not have a purpose to make the world a better place. How is that person going to feel at the end of life with no real accomplishments? So, find that passion-driven purpose, if for no other reason than your self-esteem.

Why do I still teach and work so hard at my age? Why am I writing this book? You think it's the money? As I mentioned before, LVI was sold in 2005 to a venture capital company. My wife and I did very well in the sale and we could have retired. There was no contract forcing me to stay. But I stayed and lectured. I helped to run the company.

Why? Because what I do is my passion. LVI is my baby, it's my child. I love LVI. I love it for what it stands for. I love it for what it does for society and for what it does for the doctors who come through it. Even if they didn't pay me, I'd probably still do it. I can change the life of a patient by teaching that person's dentist how to dramatically improve the patient's health and self-esteem. I can teach dentists how to help TMD patients find freedom from a lifetime of pain. I can teach dentists how to treat sleep breathing disorders, which can save patients' lives. I can also help dentists love what they do. Would that not make you feel good?

Can your life make a difference? Once again, yes!

You have the power to make someone else happy. Whatever you do in life, try to make someone happy. Change a person's life, even in a small way. Leave the world in better shape. The best feeling in the world is helping others. Whatever it takes, find a passion-driven purpose that makes you spring out of bed in the morning. Find the passion that turns work into a hobby. Find the passion that makes you happy.

> If you want to be successful, it's just this simple:
> Know what you're doing. Love what you're doing.
> And believe in what you're doing.
> **—WILL ROGERS,** American humorist

Now that you have a clear understanding about finding your passion-driven purpose, let's create your vision. That's step 2.

SUMMARY

- Determine your passion.
- Protect your passion.
- Determine who the lamplighters are in your life.
- Eliminate candle snuffers.
- Express love and gratitude.

STEP TWO
Create Your Vision

Let's hope that you have found your passion-driven purpose. And let's assume that you want to achieve that passion-driven purpose. Let's develop your vision.

> The most pathetic person in the world
> is one who has sight but has no vision.
> **—HELEN KELLER,**
> American author, political activist, and lecturer

> If you don't know where you're going,
> any road will get you there.
> **—LEWIS CARROL,** author of *Alice in Wonderland*

Shall we talk about your vision, your goals, and your dreams? Ask yourself:

- Do you know where you want to go? Most people don't.
  They just go.

- Professionally and personally, what do you want to achieve?

- What do you want to accomplish?

- Why? That's the big question. Why do you want to achieve or accomplish that? What is your reason for wanting to do that?

• Can you measure whether you're achieving your dreams? Is it money? Because if it's money, that's a problem. Money will not be enough.

Money is a great scorecard, but it's not enough to fulfill your purpose in life. Bill Gates has more money than he can possibly spend in his lifetime, but he keeps trying to improve Microsoft. Why? It's his passion. He uses money to measure the success of the company. He uses it as a scorecard.

> The greedy search for money or success will almost always lead men into unhappiness. Why? Because that kind of life makes them depend on things outside themselves.
> **—ANDREA MAUROIS,** French author

Have you heard of the Happiness Index? Researchers compared the happiness of people in relation to their salaries and income.

There was a slight increase in happiness up to $50,000 a year. After that, there was no difference in happiness based on income. This means that the $50,000 guy was just as happy as the $50 million guy. It wasn't the money.

> Perhaps the worst form of tragedy is wanting something badly, getting it, and finding it empty.
> **—HENRY KISSINGER,** former Secretary of State

Empty. That's what will happen if you're just searching for money as your goal. Think about how many successful people commit suicide. Maybe it's just that we only hear about them, but their deaths weren't caused by a lack of money. They had money, but they weren't happy.

Paradigms

When you go about trying to set your visions or your goals, you limit yourself. You do that because you have paradigms that govern what you believe you can do. I don't want you to be distracted by your perception of reality, because it's probably wrong.

> The only thing that's keeping you
> from getting what you want
> is the story you keep telling yourself.
> **—TONY ROBBINS,** American author

Your perception of what you can achieve is probably lower than what you actually can achieve. In order to attain your goal, you have to believe it, because if you don't believe it, you won't achieve it. You won't even try. You won't work at it. You won't put in the hours necessary to accomplish your goal if you think it's a waste of time—even if you want it badly.

I would have loved to play for the Lakers, but I knew I'd never make it, so I never really tried. I have a wicked three-pointer, but I'm too short at 5-foot-10 and I can't jump. My paradigm might have been correct, so I didn't waste my time trying. But who knows? Mugsy Bogues was 5-foot-4 and made the NBA—and he could dunk. He didn't listen to the people who said, "You'll never make it; you're too short."

I didn't really believe basketball fame was achievable for me, but he did! And he worked his butt off to fulfill his dream of playing in the NBA. So, you have to believe it's possible for you to achieve your dream, and that's the catch-22. If your paradigms don't allow you to believe it, you'll never achieve it. You'll never put the effort in to make that happen. You need to stretch your paradigms. But how do you stretch your paradigms? That's the difficult part. In *Star Wars*, Luke says to Yoda: "I don't believe it." And Yoda replies, "That is why you fail."

Whatever the mind of man can conceive,
it can achieve.
—W. CLEMENT STONE, businessman, philanthropist

Several years ago, *People* magazine profiled a California teenager who does remarkable things despite his disability. Ben Underwood is totally blind. He clicks to find his way around. To walk down the street with Ben is to be amazed at what he can see with his ears. Ben was just two years old when cancer claimed his eyes. Both were surgically removed.

He woke up from that surgery and said, "Mom, I can't see anymore. I can't see anymore." And his mom said, "You can't use your eyes, but you got your nose and your ears and your mouth."

From that day on, Ben has used his hearing, his touch, and his sense of smell to conquer a world of darkness. It's hard to believe how good Ben is. Somehow, Ben has mastered echolocation. It's the same way bats get around, bouncing sound waves to figure out where they are.

Nobody is going to tell Ben that something is impossible for him, because in his mind there are no barriers. His mom has done exactly the right thing with Ben: never being overprotective and never putting limits on him. I think the real story here is not his talents but his attitude. The next time you start to say, "I don't think I can do that," I want you to think about Ben. I want you to realize you have no right to sit there and doubt your ability to do something when that kid can do everything. His mother deserves a medal. What would you do if that was your kid?

Refuse to be average.
Let your heart soar as high as it will.
—A.W. TOZER, American christian pastor

Your potential is up to you. It doesn't matter what others think. It doesn't matter where you came from. It doesn't even matter what you might have believed about yourself at a previous time in your life. It's about what lies within you now and whether you can bring it out. You don't have to be what you think you have to be. It is within you. And remember, if someone else can achieve what you hope to achieve, then so can you.

In 1954, Roger Bannister broke the four-minute mile. At the time, everyone thought that would be physiologically impossible. The record of just slightly more than four minutes had been held for eleven years. The year after he broke the record, someone else did too. Then many others did as well. Today it's done all the time by high school athletes. Once it was done, that old paradigm was shattered.

> The difference between what we do and
> what we are capable of doing
> would suffice to solve most of the world's problems.
> **—GANDHI**

A black teenager at age fourteen was told by her high school counselor that she was not college material. That would have ended the dream for most people. But not for her, she believed she could do anything she wanted. She graduated from high school at sixteen. She graduated from the University of Denver at nineteen. She earned her Ph.D. at the age of twenty-six. She was a competitive figure skater and a concert pianist. She became the youngest-ever provost at Stanford, served as the youngest-ever National Security Advisor, was appointed Secretary of State, and is now one of the most powerful women to ever serve in government. I am talking about Condoleezza Rice. What if she had listened to that counselor when she was fourteen?

Remove this sentence from your vocabulary: "I can't do that." Don't let those words come out of your mouth ever again. Never say, "I can't do that."

> The greatest achievement of the human spirit
> is to live up to one's opportunities
> and make the most of one's resources.
> **—LUC DE CLAPIERS,** French writer

When my son Hunter was a sophomore in high school, he was less than ambitious, not unlike his dad at that age. Then he went to the head teacher of a program called Mock Trial.

Mock Trial is an amazing program. Kids get cases that they have to present in competition as either the attorney or witness. They have to argue both sides of the case, both the prosecution and the defense. During the competition the participants present these cases several times over at least a two-day period. It's a great program to get kids comfortable with public speaking and quick thinking. Although many of these kids decide to become lawyers, I would recommend it for any young person, regardless of what he or she wanted to do in life.

Hunter told this teacher that he was thinking of going out for Mock Trial. She said to him, "Don't bother, you won't be any good at it!"

I told my kids when they were growing up that they should not let someone discourage them—the same lesson I'm telling you here. Hunter didn't tell me what his teacher had said, so I couldn't encourage him. It was his own attitude that led him forward.

He tried out for Mock Trial, despite the teacher's horrible comment. (I don't think that woman has any business being a teacher. It's obviously not her passion.) A new teacher was the head of the program, and she believed in Hunter.

He got his friends to try out with him so at least he would have fun doing it. But something happened along the way. It turns out the previous teacher was wrong. She was very wrong. To make a long story short, Hunter won regional, state, and national awards and was named most outstanding lawyer in every competition during his junior and senior years. He excelled at contests throughout the country, competing against the best from all over the world.

He brought such recognition to the school and its Mock Trial program that they even built a complete courtroom in the school. Opposing coaches called him a superstar. One coach, who was also the head lawyer of one hundred attorneys, told me that he would have hired

Hunter on the spot if he didn't have to go to law school first. He added that Hunter was better than ninety-five of the lawyers who worked for him.

Hunter found his passion. It not only gave him focus and drive, he excelled in school for the next two years. At the time of this writing, he just graduated Summa Cum Laude from Syracuse University with a double major after only three years and won a first prize award for outstanding student in communication and rhetorical studies. He's now preparing for law school. He wants to be involved in politics and run for office someday, maybe even president. And I have no doubt that he would be a good one.

What if he had listened to that teacher? His amazing transformation may never have happened. He might still be searching for his passion, and this world might not get an amazing future president! I believe in his potential. You need to believe in yours regardless of how ridiculous it may seem at the time.

> The most absurd and reckless aspirations
> have sometimes led to extraordinary success.
> **—LUC DE CLAPIERS,** French writer

Just to show how one little thing can have a ripple effect, Hunter's decision created a dynasty at the school in the Mock Trial world. Not only did his accomplishments bring the courtroom to the school, it created an abundance of younger students who wanted to be involved in this activity, including his younger brother, Koby. Koby started the program in middle school and went on to win state championships three years in a row while in high school. Although only a senior at the time of this writing, he most likely will follow in his brother's footsteps and go to law school.

This program has created a self-confident young man in Koby, who even as a freshman, was called upon to present his school's position on a subject at a county commissioners meeting. The vote was unanimous in the school's favor and one of the adults attributed the decision to Koby's speech.

I alone cannot change the world,
but I can cast a stone across the waters
to create many ripples.
—MOTHER TERESA

Let's move to a story in which someone did listen to the teacher. In step 1, I mentioned the story about my friend Brett who wanted to be a writer but went into dentistry instead. What I didn't tell you was why he went into dentistry. Brett was top in his school in English (not just his class). He decided in ninth grade that he wanted to be a writer. His English teacher told him, without an ounce of hope, that he couldn't do it. He told Brett he wouldn't succeed. He told him that there was no money in writing and that he should pick something more practical. WOW!

So Brett gave up his dream of being a writer. Because he was also top in math, he talked to his math teacher about a career in math. The teacher's wife was a pharmacist, so he asked him about going into pharmacology. That teacher discouraged him from pursuing that career. I think the name of his high school was Negative High.

The principal's son was studying dentistry at the time, so Brett went to him. The principal was encouraging about dentistry, so that's what Brett decided to do. Obviously, there was no passion for that. Dentistry was Brett's third choice, but dentistry became his goal and he achieved it.

Brett loves people and in dentistry you are around people all day long. So, he's a happy guy, he enjoys what he does, but it was never his first passion. Brett will tell you that dentistry was not his true calling. He's ready to move on and fulfill his destiny and passion-driven purpose at fifty-six; hence, the book he wrote and published that is now for sale on Amazon.

To be what we are and to become
what we are capable of becoming
is the only end of life.
—ROBERT LOUIS STEVENSON, American author

We all doubt our abilities. We've been told not to dream too big. Our mind is our biggest obstacle to achieving our success. Most of the time these are self-imposed limitations. So think outside the box. You can do it.

There's but one cause of human failure.
And that is man's lack of faith in his true self.
—WILLIAM JAMES, psychologist and philosopher

Believe in your vision. As John Maxwell said in his book titled *Talent Is Never Enough*, "It is one thing to believe that you possess remarkable potential, it is another thing to have enough faith in yourself that you think you can fulfill it."

Whether you think you can or you can't,
either way, you are right.
—HENRY FORD, American business magnate

So now that you've identified your passion-driven purpose, do you believe it's possible? You have to believe that you can do it!

Knowing is not enough; we must apply.
Willing is not enough; we must do.
—JOHANN WOLFGANG VON GOETHE,
German writer and statesman

You probably heard the story about the lawn chair guy and the balloons. It's a true story about a man who tied a bunch of weather balloons to his lawn chair and went up, up, and away in 1982. Larry Walters always wanted to fly for the Air Force. But he wasn't allowed because of his bad eyesight. So he decided to fulfill his passion to fly another way. He bought forty-five weather balloons and filled them with helium.

You can imagine the number of people who laughed at him when he told them what he wanted to do. I'm guessing his parents gave him the mindset that he could do anything he put his mind to doing. So he put on a parachute, got a CB radio, and prepared a pellet gun, which he would use to shoot out the balloons in hopes of slowly floating to the ground. He also got a camera, and, most importantly, a beer and a sandwich. When they cut the rope, Larry took off and reached an altitude of about 16,000 feet.

But there were several big problems. He was afraid to shoot out the balloons because it might make him fall out of the chair. The wind took him over the Long Beach airport's approach corridor. Two commercial airline pilots spotted him and reported him to the FAA. After forty-five minutes of flight, he shot some of the balloons and then accidently dropped his pellet gun. He ended up stuck in a powerline causing a twenty-minute blackout in some Long Beach neighborhoods.

But that's not the end of the story. He was arrested and fined $4,000. He appealed and got it reduced to $1,500. He told the press that it had been his dream to fly for the past twenty years. It was his passion-driven purpose. The chair ended up in the San Diego Air and Space Museum.

Sadly, flying was Larry's passion-driven purpose, and other than this chair adventure, he never really pursued it. Even if he had earned a private pilot's license, the rest of the story might be brighter. Because eleven years later, at only forty-four years old, Larry killed himself leaving no suicide note.

> For true success, ask yourself these four questions:
> Why? Why not? Why not me? Why not now?
> **—JAMES ALLEN,** British writer

The Importance of a Team

Write your vision down and it becomes a goal. Create a business plan. When you have a goal and a plan, then lead your team on the path. If it's a personal goal, lead your family. Whatever the case, you can't do it alone. You could be the most amazing person in the world, but if your team sucks, you're not going to succeed. Write down your goals and read them at least every week because without vision and a goal, where are you going to lead your team, family, or friends? You need to share your goal with them, to include them in your dream.

> If your actions inspire others to dream more, learn more,
> do more and become more, you are a leader.
> **—JOHN QUINCY ADAMS,** former US President

Again, you may have all the talent in the world, but if you don't have your team behind you, you won't win the championship. In the New England Patriots' locker room, a sign says, "Individuals play the game but teams win championships." Influence your team toward a vision-driven direction through your conviction, character, and your example. Leaders believe in themselves and their cause, and they're bold in their pursuit of it. If you're not committed to your goals, you're not going to succeed. How committed are you to your vision? How committed are you to your people you've included in this dream?

> Without leadership toward implementation,
> vision is just another word for hallucination.
> **—AUTHOR UNKNOWN**

Are you willing to sacrifice to achieve your goals? Are you willing to work hard? Success does not come easy. It requires a lot of effort and going beyond what others are willing to do. The ladder to success requires effort to climb.

> There is no use whatever trying to help people
> who do not help themselves. You cannot push anyone
> up a ladder unless he is willing to climb it himself.
> **—ANDREW CARNEGIE,**
> Scottish-American industrialist and philanthropist

So are you willing to work hard for your dreams? You can't wait for it to just happen; you have to make it happen. To achieve your dreams, mediocrity will not get you there.

> No one ever attains very imminent success
> by simply doing what is required of him.
> It is the amount of excellence
> of what is over and above the required
> that determines greatness.
> **—CHARLES KENDALL ADAMS,** American educator and historian

In *Star Wars,* Obi-Wan Kenobi said, "You cannot escape your destiny." But you have to focus if you want to achieve your destiny. If you want to be successful, you must focus on what you can do and not what you can't. You have no idea what you can accomplish until you try.

> Destiny is not a matter of chance;
> it is a matter of choice.
> It is not a thing to be waited for,
> it is the thing to be achieved.
> **—WILLIAMS JENNINGS BRYAN,** American orator and politician

Write Your Business Plan

In order to make your vision or dreams into a goal, you need to write them down. And to accomplish this goal, you need to create a plan—a business plan. A plan is a cookbook that spells out what you are going to do in order to accomplish your dream. When creating your plan, you need a goal, a strategy, and a tactic. If it's a presidential election, the goal would be to win the election. The strategy may be to concentrate on the states you think you must win. The tactic is to speak about issues that are important to those voters.

Are you afraid to set a goal? Do you always ask if it's safe? Do you fear failure? Are you a follower? Do you always ask if something is popular? How many others are doing it? Do you have character? Do you always ask if it's right? Is it ethical? All these need to be considered and thought about as you write your business plan. Avoid setting paradigms that restrict you from being successful.

So how do you develop a passion-driven plan? You need to create a written path for how you are going to achieve your passion-driven purpose. Answer the following questions:

- What is your goal?
- Who is your ideal client if it's a business?
- Where will you get your customers or the help you need if it's a personal ambition?
- What outreach will you do to promote your ambition or business?
- What is your marketing plan? How are you going to let the world know you exist?
- What is your marketing budget? Do you need to borrow money for this?
- Who are you going to market to? Who is your target audience?
- How much will you charge for your services? How much do you need to succeed?
- If you need employees, how many employees do you really need? Be efficient!
- What is your ideal environment going to look like? You're going to be spending a lot of time there.

Create a one-month plan next week: goal, strategy, tactic. And then a three-month plan and then a six-month plan and then a one-year plan and then a two-year plan and then a five-year plan and then a ten-year plan, with goals, strategies, and tactics. Review it every week to see how you're doing to remind yourself of your goal, strategy, and tactics.

Here's a story about Florence Chadwick that presents a valuable lesson.

Florence Chadwick was the first woman to swim the English Channel in both directions. On the day she was trying to become the first woman to swim from Catalina Island to the California mainland, she saw nothing but a wall of fog. Her body was numb and tired. She had been swimming for nearly sixteen hours. It was a July morning in 1952, the ocean was freezing and the fog was so thick she could hardly see her support boats. Sharks that came close were driven away by rifle shots. But she struggled on hour after hour.

Those in the boats offered encouragement. They told her it wasn't much farther, but all she could see was the fog. They urged her not to quit. Not knowing how much farther she had to go, she asked to be pulled out. Sadly, she only had a half mile to go. Later, she told a reporter, "Look, I'm not excusing myself, but if I could have seen land, I might have made it." The fact that she could not see that her goal was reachable led her to quit.

Two months later she tried again and made it. This time, despite the same thick fog, she knew that somewhere behind that fog was land.

Florence Chadwick became the first woman to swim the Catalina Channel, eclipsing the man's record by two hours.

> I discovered it wasn't a matter of physical strength
> but a matter of psychological strength. The conquest lay
> within my own mind to penetrate those barriers
> of self-imposed limitations and get through to that good stuff—
> the stuff called potential, 90 percent of which we rarely use.
> **—SHARON WOOD,**
> first North American woman to climb Mount Everest

As a leader, the goals for your team must cut through the thick fog of doubt. Your goals must always be in sight. Experts on motivation disagree on a lot of things, but one thing they all agree on is that your levels of motivation are directly tied to your expected probabilities of success. In other words, if you believe you can do something, and the goals are realistic, you're likely to be highly motivated. If, however, you think you can't accomplish something and your goals are not in sight, your levels of motivation fall greatly.

> Man is what he believes.
> **—ANTON CHEKHOV,** Russian playwright

The lesson here is to continue to dream big dreams, but realize that short-term realistic goals are the real keys to success. If you just look at the final goal, it may seem unachievable. But if you break your goal into small steps, it will seem easy. If I put three hundred and sixty-five cookies on a table and told you that you had to eat all of them, you would tell me it's impossible. You wouldn't even try because it would make you sick. But you could accomplish the goal with a strategy. The strategy would be to set a timeline to accomplish the goal. So let's say you make the strategy to accomplish this goal in one year. The tactic would be to eat one cookie a day. That would be easy. The short-term goal is just one cookie a day. Then have to start. Procrastinate and you may never accomplish it.

> The secret of getting ahead is getting started.
> **—MARK TWAIN,** American writer and humorist

> There are only two mistakes one can make
> along the road to truth: not going all the way,
> and not starting.
> **—GAUTAMA BUDDHA**

Create your vision and then do it with baby steps. Make it a daily process and your task becomes a habit.

> We are what we repeatedly do.
> **—ARISTOTLE,** Ancient Greek philosopher

You should set your goals out of your comfort zone. If it's not a stretch, then you're not pushing yourself. You should push your limits to reach the heights of what you can be.

> Few men during their lifetime
> come anywhere near exhausting the resources
> dwelling within them. There are deep wells of strength
> that are never used.
> **—ADMIRAL RICHARD BYRD,** American naval officer

So now you have your purpose determined. You are protecting it while your heart is filled with love and gratitude. You've created your business plan, setting out the goal, strategy, and tactics to get there. The biggest problem for most people at this point is their attitude, which can prevent them from achieving their goals. So let's deal with that aspect of achieving your passion-driven purpose next.

SUMMARY

- Widen your paradigms.
- Create your vision.
- What is your goal?
- What is your strategy?
- What is your tactic?
- Make a business plan.

STEP THREE
Adjust Your Attitude—It's Everything

Life is not about what happens, it's about your perspective on what happened. You may not be able to change what happened, but you can always choose to change the way you decide to act on what happened. Think about that. Your attitude is the only thing in life that you have complete control over. Nobody can do that for you. You can choose to have a positive, a negative, an optimistic, or a pessimistic attitude. It's your choice.

> Nothing can stop the man
> with the right mental attitude from achieving his goal;
> nothing on earth can help the man
> with the wrong mental attitude.
> **—THOMAS JEFFERSON,**
> American founding father and president

Almost every successful person that I've seen has a positive attitude. Success is more attitude than aptitude.

> The greatest discovery of my generation
> is that human beings can alter their lives
> by altering their attitudes of mind.
> **—WILLIAM JAMES,** American philosopher

You can blame problems or events on other people, but it's your decision to allow them to influence you in that direction. Losers spend time gathering data to justify their decisions, choices, and failures rather than changing their attitude. And most of the time, all it takes is a little attitude adjustment. Without that, people can make really bad decisions.

W. Mitchell was involved in a motorcycle accident that left him burned over 75 percent of his body. His fingers melted off. His face was badly burned. He said he looked like a monster, totally scarred. But it didn't change his attitude. He came back and started loving life even though he looked like a self-described monster. He made a decision, "I don't care whether people look at me as a monster. I know what I am."

He decided to live life to the fullest and took flying lessons. It was hard because he had no fingers. Life was going great until he crashed the plane, which left him paralyzed. Now he's in a wheelchair.

Most people would have been depressed, even suicidal. But the guy has the greatest positive attitude. He's an inspiration of positivity. His passion-driven purpose has been to lecture around the world spreading his message of positivity: "It's not what happens to you, it's what you do about it."

> The mind is everything. What you think, you become.
> **—GAUTAMA BUDDHA**

The next time you think about how bad you have it, think of Mitchell and think how positive he is and what he's done with his life. Everything you do in life is your choice. That's especially true at work and, for kids, at school. You choose how you conduct yourself; you choose how you treat others; you choose your attitude; you choose how to respond to stress and adversity; you choose the levels of honesty and the integrity you display; you choose whether to take your responsibilities seriously or not. Remember that there are consequences to each choice we make. Bad choices usually have bad consequences.

Blaming others for your poor choices is a waste of time. The it's-someone-else's-fault victim mentality is a path to nowhere. Want to be successful? Take responsibility for yourself and your choices and choose well because that choice will determine the outcome. Stop blaming others. Make a decision!

> The golden opportunity you're seeking is in yourself.
> It is not in your environment; it is not in luck or chance,
> or the help of others, it is in yourself alone.
> **—ORISON MARDEN,** American inspirational author

Positive Attitude

Do you have a positive attitude? Do you look at the silver lining in the cloud or do you look at the cloud in a silver lining?

There is story on the Internet called "Two Choices." I have searched to find the original source, but all references say the author is unknown. Its message is so powerful I felt it important to include it in this book.

You all have two choices. Jerry is the manager of a restaurant. He's always in a good mood. When someone asks him how he is doing, he always replies, "If I were any better, I would be twins." Many of the waiters at his restaurant quit their jobs when Jerry changed jobs, so they could follow him around from restaurant to restaurant. Why? Because Jerry was a natural motivator.

If an employee was having a bad day, Jerry was always there, telling them how to look on the positive side of the situation. Seeing this style really made me curious. So one day, I went up to Jerry and I asked him, "I don't get it. No one can be a positive person all the time. How do you do it?"

Jerry replied, "Each morning, I wake up and say to myself, 'I have two choices today. I can choose to be in a good mood or I can choose to be in a bad mood.' I always choose to be in a good mood. Each time something bad happens, I can choose to be a victim or I can choose to learn from it. I always choose to learn from it. Every time someone comes to me complaining, I can choose to accept their complaining or I can point out the positive side of life. I always choose the positive side of life."

"But it's not always that easy," I protested.

"Yes, it is," Jerry said. "Life is all about choices. When you cut away all the junk, every situation is a choice. You choose how you react to the situations. You choose how people will affect your mood. You choose to be in a good mood or a bad mood. It's your choice how you live your life."

Several years later, I heard that Jerry accidentally did something you were never supposed to do in the restaurant business. He left the back door of his restaurant open. And in the morning, he was robbed by three armed men. While Jerry tried to open the safe, his hands, shaking from nervousness, slipped off the combination. The robbers panicked and shot him. Luckily, Jerry was found quickly and rushed to the hospital.

After eighteen hours of surgery and weeks of intensive care, Jerry was released from the hospital with fragments of the bullets in his body. I saw Jerry about six months after the accident. When I asked him how he was, he replied, "If I was even better, I'd be twins. Want to see my scars?"

I declined to see his wounds but did ask him what had gone through his mind as the robbery took place.

"The first thing that went through my mind was that I should have locked the back door," Jerry replied. "Then after they shot me as I lay on the floor, I remember that I had two choices: I could choose to live or I could choose to die. I chose to live."

"Weren't you scared?" I asked.

Jerry continued, "The paramedics were great. They kept telling me I was going to be fine. But when they wheeled me into the emergency room and I saw the expression on the faces of the doctors and nurses, I got really scared. In their eyes I read, 'He's a dead man.' I knew I needed to take action."

"What did you do?" I asked.

"Well, there was a big nurse shouting questions at me and she asked if I was allergic to anything. 'Yes, to bullets,' I replied. Over their laughter, I told them, 'I'm choosing to live, please operate on me as if I am alive, not dead.'"

Jerry lived, thanks to the skill of his doctors but also because of his amazing attitude. Every day you have the choice to either enjoy your life or to hate it. The only thing that no one can control or take away from you is your attitude. So if you can take care of that, everything else in life becomes much easier.

> For success, attitude
> is equally as important as ability.
> **—WALTER SCOTT,** Scottish novelist and poet

Think of yourself, not in terms of all your problems, but with your most positive possibilities. Don't think of your regrets or disappointments, but learn from them to create positive results. The way you think of yourself and your future can become your reality. If you see yourself being the best you can be, you can achieve it. See yourself as this positive, happy person and you may become that person in no time.

If you are a golf fan, you might hear that many of the pros visualize the ball doing exactly what they want it to do before they hit it. Jason Day closes his eyes to visualize his shot and then hits it. If you visualize yourself failing, you will. (If the water hazard becomes your fear, for example, your ball will surely end up in the water.)

> What concerns me is not the way things are
> but rather the way people think things are.
> **—EPICTETUS,** Greek stoic philosopher

Many of you have read the book or have seen the movie *The Secret*. I'm not a fan. The biggest secret in life is that there is no secret. Whatever your dreams and goals are, you can get there only if you are willing to work hard. Positive thoughts are great, but they are not enough. I know many people who say that all we need are positive thoughts, but that's not enough. If you rely only on positive thoughts for success, you will be positively disappointed.

I hear it all the time. "I'm just not lucky like you or him or her, right? I'm still waiting for my ship to come in." It's not about luck. You have to go after your dreams and goals. All the talent in the world won't lead to success without initiative. Just do something. Start today.

> You cannot escape the responsibility
> of tomorrow by avoiding it today.
> **—ABRAHAM LINCOLN,** American president

If you want your life to be a magnificent story, then realize that you're its author. Every day get up and decide to write a new chapter to that story. Don't procrastinate. Let this book be the impetus to get off your butt and start pursuing your passion-driven purpose!

> He slept beneath the moon,
> he basked beneath the sun,
> he lived the life of going to do,
> and died with nothing done.
> **—JAMES ALBERY,** English dramatist

We all have dreams, but sometimes we never act on them. I'm guilty of this as well. It's taken me too many years to finally write this book. To achieve my tasks, I create checklists of things I need to do. Write a priority list and compare that with your talent and passion list. What can you do to align them? And then take the first step to where you want to go. Consider this your opportunity to finally getting started on your journey.

> To succeed, jump as quickly at opportunities
> as you do at conclusions.
> **—BENJAMIN FRANKLIN,**
> American president, inventor, and founding father

You know, most people are good at jumping to conclusions. But jump at the opportunities as well. If you don't take the initiative, you're guaranteed to fail.

> Nothing is so fatiguing as the
> hanging on of an uncompleted task.
> **—WILLIAM JAMES,** American philosopher

Don't wait for the perfect time to act because that perfect time may never come.

> Do what you can,
> with what you have,
> where you are.
> **—THEODORE ROOSEVELT,** American president

Don't procrastinate. Do you have a decision that you should be making right now? Do you have a problem you need to solve? Do you have a project that you should be starting? A goal you should be reaching? An opportunity you should be seizing? A dream you should be fulfilling? Then just do it with a positive attitude.

> He who deliberates fully before taking one step
> will spend his entire life on one leg.
> **—CHINESE PROVERB**

Negative Attitude

Negativity: I call it the success-destroying virus. You have to eliminate negativity. It's there in all of us but you need to suppress it. Like a computer virus, negativity will spread throughout your life and the people around you. Positive people will become negative and the company can crash. If you have a negative coworker now, try to keep the negativity from spreading. It's essential to remove the virus of negativity.

> No pessimist ever discovered the secret of the stars,
> or sailed to an uncharted land or opened a new doorway
> for the human spirit.
> **—HELEN KELLER,**
> American author, political activist, and lecturer

Negativity is my pet peeve. Most of my friends know I can't stand negativity. I can't stand whiny, complaining people because I know it's their choice. There's a lot of "yeah, buts" out there.

Let's talk about the "yeah, buts." You hear it all the time: Yeah, but we can't do that. Yeah, but we don't have those kinds of clients. Yeah, but that's not me. Yeah, but our area isn't like that. Yeah, but the economy isn't good now. Yeah, but that's not realistic.

> Blessed is he who expects nothing
> for he shall never be disappointed.
> **—BENJAMIN FRANKLIN,**
> American president, inventor, and founding father

If you want to achieve something, you have to be willing to be disappointed. Disappointment is going to happen. You're never going to be ecstatic about the results all the time. And if you don't do something for fear of being disappointed, then you'll never accomplish your goals.

The only limit to our realization of tomorrow
will be our doubts of today.
—FRANKLIN ROOSEVELT, American president

In his book, *The Last Lecture,* Randy Pausch wrote: "Too many people go through life complaining about their problems. I've always believed that if you took one-tenth the energy you put into complaining and applied it to solving the problem, you'd be surprised by how well things can work out."

Isn't that great? He's 100 percent right.

It is better to light a candle
than to curse the darkness.
—ELEANOR ROOSEVELT, first lady

Look for the silver lining. There's a story about four worms and a lesson. A minister has decided that a visual demonstration would add emphasis to a Sunday sermon. Four worms were placed into four separate jars. The first worm was put in a container of alcohol. The second worm was put in a container of cigarette smoke. The third worm was put into a container of chocolate syrup. And then the fourth worm was put into a container of good clean soil. At the conclusion of the sermon, the minister reported the following results.

The first worm in alcohol, dead; the second worm in cigarette smoke, dead; the third worm in chocolate syrup, dead; the fourth worm in good clean soil, alive. So the minister asked the congregation, "What can you learn from this demonstration?"

Maxine, the optimist, was sitting in the back quickly raised her hand and said, "As long as you drink, smoke, and eat chocolate, you won't have worms."

You see? Whatever happens, look for the positive. A recent study found that the average American walks about nine hundred miles a year and another study found Americans drink on average twenty-two gallons of alcohol a year. How can we make that positive?

Well, that means on average, Americans get about 42 miles to the gallon. That's pretty damn good.

I know life is not fair. But it's what you do about that unfairness that will determine your future.

> Do not dwell in the past, do not dream of the future,
> concentrate the mind on the present moment.
> **—GAUTAMA BUDDHA**

Bad choices usually have bad consequences, and blaming others for your poor choices is a waste of time. I have the pleasure of helping dentists help their patients. But many don't want my help for reasons such as ego, pride or arrogance. And when they can't help their patients, they blame others . . . perhaps the patient, or the lab, or look for other reasons than their work causing the problems. The it's-someone-else's-fault victim mentality is a sure path to fail. Want to be truly successful? Take responsibility for yourself and your choices and choose well.

> If your deeds are unsuccessful,
> seek the reason in yourself.
> When your own person is correct,
> the whole world will turn to you.
> **—MENCIUS,** Chinese philosopher

We are the creators of our own stories, not the victims of it. Viktor Frankl was a prisoner in Auschwitz. His family was murdered. In his book *Man's Search for Meaning* he says, "You are not a victim as long as you have choices." And that's the one thing somebody can't take from you. How someone could come out of the Holocaust with the positive attitude he had is amazing. He witnessed the worst of the worst, the darkest evil that exists, and yet he was determined to not let that experience take away his spirit and positive attitude. Again, your attitude is the only thing you have complete control over.

Next time you start getting negative; remind yourself that you're allowing someone else to affect you and your attitude when you actually have complete control over that.

> Most folks are about as happy
> as they make up their minds to be.
> **—ABRAHAM LINCOLN,** American president

If you are a negative person right now, just admit it. Denying it isn't going to help. A lot of you have negative attitudes. Some of my friends have negative attitudes. Are you in denial? Do you say, "I don't have a negative attitude, it's just that everyone is against me and life sucks." Think about that.

It's your choice to be a Tigger or in Eeyore. For those of you who don't know Winnie the Pooh, Tigger was the tiger who said, "Oh, hey, what a great day." Always happy, right? And Eeyore would walk around, "Oh, woe is me. What's going to happen to me today?"

So at LVI, for the last eighteen years, we've done something fun at our team meetings. At first we would give out Tigger and Eeyore awards. We'd give the Tigger awards to those with the positive, happy attitudes, and we pick somebody who was always in a bad mood or grumpy, and we'd give that person the Eeyore award. But the Eeyore always went to the same guy. When he left the company, we gave it to him to take and retired the Eeyore because it was a negative reinforcement.

Positive reinforcement is a much better way to change behavior. So now we just give Tigger Awards. Every month, we give two Tigger Awards to our employees. So choose to be a Tigger. Wake up each morning in a happy mood ready to start the day. Don't be an Eeyore, because the world is awesome. And if you're not enjoying it, you're making a huge mistake.

There is one attitude that deserved a chapter all itself. So the next chapter is dedicated to a destructive attitude: jealousy.

SUMMARY

- What is your current attitude?

- Work on being positive.

- Eliminate negative thoughts.

- Set up goals to spread positivity in your office and family.

Step Four
Eliminate Jealousy

Let's define jealousy.

The dictionary says:

1. Jealous resentment against a rival, a person enjoying success or advantage, etc., or against another's success or advantage itself.

2. Mental uneasiness from suspicion or fear of rivalry, unfaithfulness, etc., as in love or aims.

3. Vigilance in maintaining or guarding something.

4. Jealous feeling, disposition, state, or mood.

From the website of *Psychology Today*:

Understanding Jealousy: Jealousy is a complex emotion that encompasses feelings ranging from fear of abandonment to rage and humiliation. Jealousy strikes both men and women and is most typically aroused when a person perceives a threat to a valued relationship from a third party. The threat may be real or perceived. It is not limited to romantic relationships but also can arise among siblings competing for parental attention or in friendships. Jealousy is distinguished from envy in that jealousy always involves a third party seen as a rival for affection. Envy occurs between two people and is best summed up as "I want what you have." Although jealousy is a painful emotional experience, evolutionary psychologists regard it not as an emotion to be suppressed but as one to heed—it is a signal, a wake-up call, that a valued relationship is in danger and steps need to be taken to regain the affection of one's mate or friend. In this regard, jealousy is a necessary emotion because it preserves social bonds. It motivates people to engage in behaviors that maintain an important relationship.

I don't believe this to be the case. I've seen too many people's lives and careers ruined because of jealousy. In my view and from my life experiences, jealousy is rarely a good thing. It's not something that should be seen as a motivation but as something everyone should work to avoid. Jealousy is just destructive.

Many people are hampered by jealousy. It will destroy you—not the person you're jealous of. Jealous people spend energy on destroying others, not on building themselves or working on their weaknesses. Jealousy is a side effect of a mindset that's rooted in scarcity. Somebody has something that you can't have. Maybe you believe the fact that they have it means that you can't have it. The truth is, it doesn't mean you can't.

Jealousy results from the notion that another person's success or happiness somehow diminishes your own. It doesn't. The happiest thing for me would be for all of you to be more successful than me. Why? Because I'm comfortable with what I have and grateful for the love and gratitude I have in my life. If you were happy, why would I ever not want that for you? I want to be around happy and positive people, so why would I be jealous of people who I like being around?

If you could look at the world through the lens of abundance instead of scarcity, then it would be very difficult for you to be jealous. Let me give you an example.

Let's assume there is a rich guy in your town. Everyone is jealous of him. But that rich guy is going to spend money, and he's going to spend it with you. And what happens when he spends it with you?

You become richer.

And then you spend the money with someone else, and then that person becomes richer.

And then that person spends the money with another guy, and then that guy becomes richer.

And it keeps going until we have all these rich people. But it doesn't stop there. Those people start spending money with each other and they all get richer.

It's why tax cuts work. It puts money in the hands of the people who spend it. But each dollar isn't just spent once. One person spends it, and then the guy who received payment spends the money, and on and on. It's eventually passed to millions, and millions benefit.

Throughout my career, people have been jealous of me because of my success.

- They say things like, "His kids are too good." Well they're right about that. I have great kids.

- "His wife is too smart and too beautiful." Well they're right about that, too, she's amazing.

- "He has too nice of a house. He flies his own airplane. He needs to be brought down."

Instead of trying to eliminate me, they should be trying to emulate me. Instead of trying so hard to destroy, they would have been better off trying to learn from me.

- "He gets very little sleep," somebody says. "Yeah, but I want my sleep."

- "He works hard even on the weekends," one of my defenders would say. "Yeah, but I want my play time and don't want to work that hard."

- "He empowers others," my friend says to them. "Yeah, but I don't have time for that. It's hard enough to empower myself."

"He's just too lucky; he needs to be brought down and I'm going to work hard at bringing him down."

Sadly, I can remember only four people in my life who have apologized to me after they did bad things to me or said bad things about me. I know it's hard to apologize, but it shouldn't be hard. I've forgiven them.

I suffered from jealousy when I was a younger. I felt the competitiveness with other dentists—an apparent disease that affects my profession. If someone was successful or well-known, I would find reasons to say something negative about them. At a society dinner, someone mentioned a dentist, and I said something negative not knowing who he was. He was sitting at the table with us. I talked my way out of it, but it made me realize that my jealousy was destructive and evil.

> The jealous are possessed by a mad devil
> and a dull spirit at the same time.
> **—JOHANN KASPAR LAVATER,** Swiss poet, writer, philosopher

I wish someone had talked to me back then like I'm talking to you right now. I was not happy being a dentist and my unhappiness was misdirected. I hated the work so much that I looked at those who were successful or happy as the enemy. They weren't. I was my own enemy.

The next time you are about to say something negative about someone, ask yourself:

- Is it true?

- Is it unkind?

- Does it serve a purpose?

If it's true and it serves a purpose, let's say to prevent someone from hiring an unethical person or going into business with a difficult person, then say it. But if there is no reason to say it, even if it's true, then don't do it. If you have done something bad, free yourself by apologizing. It's never too late.

People who spend energy trying to bring someone down destroy themselves in the process. Don't do it. James 3:16 says, "For where jealousy and selfish ambition exists, there is disorder and every evil thing." The results of your jealous actions will backfire. Perhaps there may be something to karma. Most of the people who were jealous of me and tried hard to hurt me have been negatively affected in their lives. None of them were really successful, either in their attempt to bring down LVI or in their efforts to compete against me. In fact, most of them failed in achieving their goals. They just made LVI stronger because I would take that negative energy and work hard to turn it into positive results. Next time it happens to you, do the same.

> The jealous are troublesome to others,
> but a torment to themselves.
> **—WILLIAM PENN,** Quaker and founder of Pennsylvania

How do you ignore the evils of those who are jealous? The answer isn't easy, but it is simple. Instead of spending the energy to get revenge, apply the same amount of time and energy to work on your passion-driven purpose. When I faced a jealous attack during the early days of LVI, a good friend (let's call him Ronald Jackson) told me to let my success be my answer. After twenty-three years of LVI's amazing success story, it's apparent I listened to him. Thanks, Ron. Love and gratitude.

> Jealousy is the tribute mediocrity pays to genius.
> **—BISHOP FULTON J. SHEEN,** American theologian

When we have thoughts of jealousy or feelings of envy, our lives will be hampered by feelings of worthlessness. No good action comes from an evil, vengeful, and jealous spirit. Dealing with your jealousy is essential. If you're currently struggling with jealousy I recommend you search your heart. There is a reason why jealousy is plaguing you. It's usually caused by something inside you that you're upset about.

In my case, I was internally unhappy and hated dentistry. Perhaps you'll need to talk to someone who can get it out of you. It's critically important to lead a happy and healthy life.

> As iron is eaten away by rust,
> so the envious are consumed by their own passion.
> **—ANTISTHENES**, Greek philosopher

Ask yourself why you would be jealous of a person's success and happiness. As I mentioned earlier, if everyone was successful and happy, we wouldn't have evil. When was the last time you heard about a happy person doing anything evil? I can't think of any. People do evil things because they are not content with themselves. They are not at peace with themselves. Deep inside they really don't like who they are. They can change, but are so filled with evil and hate that they won't. They just try to justify their evil actions.

I want everyone to be happy and to find their passion-driven purpose. You could say that's my purpose in life. When people around me are happy and fulfilled, they naturally spread those feelings to others. I'd rather be surrounded by people who are doing better than I am than by people who are unhappy. Seeing people exceed my capabilities doesn't make me jealous; it inspires me.

> He is a wise man who does not grieve
> for the things which he has not,
> but rejoices for those which he has.
> **—EPICTETUS**, Greek stoic philosopher

Jealousy will throw rocks on the ice of success making it more difficult to skate through life. Please, for your own happiness, eliminate jealousy from your life.

Let's end this rather serious and somber chapter with a little humor.

My wife's jealousy is getting ridiculous.
The other day she looked at my calendar
and wanted to know who May was.
—RODNEY DANGERFIELD,
American stand-up comedian and actor

Even if you're not a jealous type, there is something else that will prevent you from achieving your passion-driven purpose: irrational fear. Let's go to the next chapter to see if we can eliminate that from your life.

SUMMARY

- If you are a jealous person, work on it.
- What is the real reason you're jealous?
- It's you, not them.
- Think love and gratitude.
- Be grateful for what you have.
- Eliminate jealousy from your life.

STEP FIVE
Control Irrational Fears that Prevent Success

A re you hampered by fear? Are your fears preventing you from being successful? Are you passing this on to your children?

> What would life be if we had
> no courage to attempt anything?
> **—VINCENT VAN GOGH,** artist

Everyone has fears, but to succeed you need to control your fears and
not allow them to control you.

There are good fears, fears you should have. Those are rational
fears. But there are also many irrational fears. It is hard for a person with
irrational fears to be successful.

Understanding Rational Fears

Afraid to run across a busy freeway? That's a rational fear. Being afraid
to jump off a sixty-foot cliff is obviously a rational fear. Being afraid to
stick a toothpick in your eye is obviously a rational fear. To be afraid of
fighting with Mike Tyson is a rational fear (for most of us). Life is loaded
with rational fears. They are good because they keep us safe and alive.

There is an inherent risk in everything we do. Just sitting in your
house, there is an inherent risk. Walking down the sidewalk on a sunny

day has a risk. A car can jump the curb and kill you. A brick could fall from a building. Something could fall from the sky. But it's not likely to happen.

And then there are operational risks. Those are risks caused by our own decisions and actions in pursuit of a goal or objective. We all need to take operational risks. We will only take on operational risk by measuring the anticipated consequences of our actions against the potential gains. We do this every day.

> Take risks: if you win, you will be happy;
> if you lose, you will be wise.
> **—ANONYMOUS**

A professional surfer wants to surf the giant wave because doing it would be worth it. As one who's never surfed before, I would not take this risk. It wouldn't be worth it because the risk would be far greater than the reward. I probably wouldn't survive. Sometimes we take extraordinary risks because the gains justify the risk. Sometimes moderate gains warrant moderate risks. Whatever the case, we all bring a set of life experiences that influence how we see and manage risk.

For most, our approach to risk changes over time with experience and age. Young people take all kinds of risks. But when we get married and have a child, we avoid risks. Why? Because we're afraid of what could happen to that kid if something happens to us. It's the nesting instinct. I'm not saying it's an irrational risk or a wrong decision, just that it's there. For those of you whose kids are now grown, start taking risks again. They'll be fine. Go have some fun!

Every decision in life is about risk versus reward. How great is the risk? How great is the reward? Is the reward worth the risk? The thrill of soaring on a zipline, for example, always begins with the fear of falling. My favorite line is, you don't really feel alive until you're close to death.

So what are some examples of irrational fears?

- Fear of water

- Fear of public speaking

- Fear of failing

- Fear of change

- Fear of trying something new

- Fear of being wrong

- Fear of crowds

Overcome the Most Common Irrational Fear—Flying

I want to talk about a common irrational fear because it's hampering many people from being as successful as they can be. It's the fear of flying. I'm going to prove that it's an irrational fear.

Do you avoid meetings, family events, vacations, or business courses that would make you better at what you do because you are afraid to fly? Many people drive hours and hours because they are afraid to fly. Do you resist going to see a site, experience something new, or visit family and friends because you're afraid to fly? Many people do.

According to the National Institute of Mental Health, 19.6 million Americans have a fear of flying. In fact, 6.5 percent of Americans have a fear of flying so intense that it qualifies as a phobia or anxiety disorder. This is totally irrational.

Let's look at some facts that prove my point.

In 2000, the world's commercial jet airlines carried approximately 1.09 billion people on eighteen million flights while suffering only twenty fatal accidents. That makes your chance of dying in a plane crash 0.00000018 percent. And it's become safer ever since.

In the United States, it's twenty-two times safer to fly in a commercial jet than to travel by car. Measured in deaths per mile, American commercial airline flights are twenty-two times safer than car travel.

More people die in three months of traffic accidents than in forty years of flying on commercial jets. More Americans die each year falling from ladders, drowning in bathtubs, and freezing to death than by flying. According to the *Air & Space* magazine transportation accident statistics, the one-year odds of dying in a plane accident are 501,000 to 1. The lifetime chance of dying in a plane is 6,438 to 1.

Your odds of dying in a bike accident are much greater than flying in an airplane. Occupants of all terrain or off-road motor vehicles are twice as likely to die than those in an airplane.

Just simple falling is way more fatal than flying. It's 15,000 to 1 every year that you'll die from a fall versus 501,000 to 1 in an airplane. Falls involving a bed, chair, or other furniture and you're more likely to die from that than an airplane.

Drowning in a submersion well or falling into a swimming pool, you're more likely to die from that than flying in an airplane.

The only one that is a little bit safer, and it's just a little bit safer, is accidental suffocation or strangulation in bed. How in the hell is that going to happen? You got twisted in your robe tie? And that's only slightly safer than flying.

Even inhalation and ingestion of food causing obstruction of breathing is way more dangerous than flying. You didn't stop eating did you?

Tobacco's the number one cause of death, and then diet/activity patterns, and then alcohol, and then microbial agents, and then toxic agents, then firearms, then sexual behavior, then motor vehicles, and then illicit use of drugs. Flying is not even on the list.

And if you get to just accidental deaths, the number one cause of death is motor vehicle accidents. And then falls, and then poisoning, and drowning, and fires, and surgical complications, and land transport and firearms and then other non-transportation accidents. Aviation does not even make that list either.

You want to know a weird fact? More people are killed by donkeys annually than by airplane crashes. For God's sake, stay away from donkeys.

So why are people so afraid of airplanes? Because the news reports every airplane crash. If a small plane crashed today in Orlando, it will be in your local news no matter where you live. It will even be on national news. Just one crash! So everybody thinks it happens all the time because media reports it all the time. If a car crashes in Orlando, it probably won't even make the local news there.

The average number of people in the air right this minute while you're reading this book is around 61,000 people.

Fear of flying is an irrational fear based on emotions. What's the worst thing that can happen anyway? You die. Well, if you're religious, then you get to go to heaven, the place that you really believe you're meant to be. For everybody who's religious, that's a good thing isn't it? And if you're not a believer and you're right, then you'll never know that you died. So what difference does it make?

Let me give you a hypothetical situation to measure your fear. Be honest about answering this.

You have an hour-long flight for a non-essential trip. There's no real reason for you to get on this plane because it wouldn't be a big deal if you didn't go. If you knew in advance that the plane would suddenly drop 10,000 feet at a rate of 20,000 feet a minute, would you go?

I didn't think so. But for those who said you would still go, let's make it worse. What if you knew the pilot would intentionally dive the airplane fifteen times during your flight? Now would you get on that plane?

I didn't think so. But what if you knew there were more than eight thousand people that had paid $4,000 for this hour-long flight, knowing all this was going to happen?

Well, I did it. It's called Zero Gravity Flight. It was one of the most fun things I've ever done. Dropping fast puts you in zero gravity. You get to experience what the astronauts experience in space. The inside of the plane was completely padded. I had a blast releasing M&Ms and watching them float as I tried to eat them. It was fun to watch a splash of water float as I hovered nearby and gulped it down. I would spin in the air like a top. I would recommend the experience to anyone.

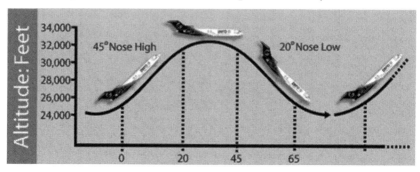

So was your initial fear about this flight rational or irrational? It was an irrational fear because you didn't know the whole story about the precautions that made it safe and fun. If you had known about those precautions, would you have taken the flight? Even if it were free? If not, then you're letting an irrational fear prevent you from an amazing life experience.

Maybe you'll fly in a commercial airline but you are afraid to fly in a small private plane. Is that rational or irrational? Flying in any sort of plane is still far safer and less dangerous than driving in a car. There are only sixteen fatal accidents per million hours of general aviation. I fly my own plane and it's one of my passions.

Would you jump out of an airplane? Is it irrational to do so? The United States Parachute Association members reported making nearly 2.2 million jumps with only twenty-seven fatalities. Nevertheless, skydiving scared me to death. I said I would never do it.

But I needed to overcome this irrational fear, so I decided to do it. The day before my jump, a pertinent news story emerged: "Two Killed in Skydiving Accident." Now the pessimist would have said, "I'm not going." He would see the story as a divine warning or omen to not jump. But being the optimist, I said to my wife, "What are the chances it will now happen two days in a row?" Statistically the odds were in my favor.

So I jumped. And I was scared. The jump was from fifteen thousand feet. We fell at 120 miles an hour. The only part that was scary was leaving the airplane. After that it was like being in a wind tunnel. It was a rush, an amazing rush. When we landed, my legs were so weak I couldn't easily get up. But I felt so good. I was able to conquer my fear. I would do it again. The point is, you need to do stuff like this. You need to go beyond your envelope of comfort.

Are you afraid to swim in the ocean? If you knew there were sharks in your location, would you go in? Well, I went scuba diving with sharks in Bora Bora. I figured if people dive to see these sharks every day, they must be feeding these sharks really well or something. I figured they wouldn't take divers in the water if it was dangerous. It was irrational for me to think that it wouldn't be safe. And it was amazing. I admit that one shark waited a bit too long before he swam away from me, but seeing it that close was so cool.

Is it rational to fear climbing to the top of a bridge? My wife, Heidi, and I climbed to the top of the Sydney Harbor Bridge. It would have been irrational to be afraid because we were chained to the bridge by a sliding cable. You can't fall, and if you could, you'd hang there by the cable. Yet I still know many who are afraid to enjoy this adventure. If you are ever in Sydney, I recommend that you do the bridge climb.

Fear of roller coasters is another irrational fear. Would they have roller coasters all over the world if people died? My boys and I are roller coaster freaks! My son Koby's first roller coaster scared him to death. People looked at me as if I should be turned in to Child Protective Services for taking him. But when he got off the roller coaster, he said, "Let's do it again." The next year, when he was only seven, he went on a terrifying one with me and he handled it like a champ.

My middle son, Hunter, was afraid to go on a scary roller coaster when he was ten. I told him I would give him $10 if he went with me. As we were waiting in line, he was sweating and his heart was beating out of his chest. I could literally see it. People in line were cracking up. But he was brave and went on the ride with me. I think I could hear his heart beat before it took off. The coaster was amazing! He got off, I gave him the ten bucks, and he said, of course, "Let's do it again." Fortunately, my wife also likes roller coasters, so it's a family adventure. My boys were afraid at first, but I helped them realize their fear was irrational. Not only did they survive, they had a great time and became coaster fanatics.

> You gain strength, courage and confidence
> by every experience in which you really stop to look fear in the face.
> You must do things which you think you cannot do.
> **—ELEANOR ROOSEVELT,** former first lady

The problem with adults is they have grown up. They lose the enthusiasm and zest for life they had as a kid. Do you remember what you felt like as a kid? Life was an amazing world of new adventures. Wouldn't you like to have that back? People miss out on the thrills of life itself by being too adult. It's the I'm-too-serious-for-that attitude. "I can't do that I'm an adult, that's just for kids." And because of that, the excitement of life is lost.

In a song by John Cougar Mellencamp called "Jack & Diane" the chorus talks about how life goes on long after the thrill of living is gone. And every time I hear that song, I am saddened because the lyrics fit so many people. Don't let that happen. Why would you ever want to grow up, if that's how you're going to feel about life? Why would you not want to be a kid for the rest of your life? Let that kid in you come out again. Life is to be enjoyed!

I have in my wallet something my son Hunter wrote in elementary school. The kids in his class were asked to write a report for Father's Day about their father. He wrote a long essay. The teachers picked the good ones and sent them to the local newspaper, where the lines were edited and published.

This is what Hunter wrote about me: "My dad is great from every aspect. Even as a high schooler he started to do great things. He takes time out of his day to coach me and my brother's teams in soccer, baseball, and basketball. He always makes me laugh and even when I'm sad. He also is just a big kid."

The last sentence is my second favorite line (they edited out my favorite one). It goes on, "He'll play video games with me, try to push my older brother into our pool. He plays sports with me and does everything with me. He is great." The line that they cut out was, "He is my best friend." Hunter is twenty-two now, but I hope he still feels the same.

I laminated the clipping and keep it in my wallet. Thank you, Hunter. I love you.

Make Your Life a Daring Adventure

I want to tell you a story about "the trip of a lifetime." Other than my work, my passions are family, flying (I'm a private pilot), roller coasters, and adventure. So my wife and I took our three boys on a passion-filled trip. For twenty-three days we flew around the country in our small plane. I admit that I was nervous because our trip was so dependent on the weather. I was flying into many unfamiliar airports. Long flights at high altitudes made we worry about icing—no friend to planes. But I wanted to mix the amazing natural wonders our country had to offer with a roller coaster/adventuresome time.

That trip modeled what I'm telling you to do in this book. I set out my plan. The plan was to take a great trip before my oldest left for college. We would probably never get to do something like this again. My strategy was to mix fun with amazing sights. The tactic was to make each leg of the trip a reasonable length while making sure the stop was worthwhile. I flew into each airport on my simulator in advance of the trip to get some familiarity with the approaches and airport layouts. I had backup plans just in case we couldn't get into certain airports. We had our lodging and car rentals all set. The plan was perfectly organized. The strategy and tactics were specified for each location and in place. The desire was there—something I had thought about and wanted to do for a long time.

We went to Yellowstone and saw its amazing and beautiful natural wonders; Mount Rushmore and the beautiful Black Hills; Wisconsin Dells, the best water parks in the country; Cedar Point for the greatest roller coaster park in the world; Niagara Falls, the Maid of the Mist and a boat ride behind the falls. We visited with friends on an island off Maine (spectacular beauty); Hershey, Pennsylvania, for another roller coaster park; Pidgeon Forge, Tennessee, to ride inside a big Zorb ball down the side of a mountain; Jacksonville Beach and Destin to enjoy the warm waters of the Atlantic and the Gulf of Mexico. Then we flew to Dallas to Six Flags Roller Coaster Park; Durango to dirt bike, to float down a freezing river, and to explore the great outdoors of the Rockies; Sedona to experience the Pink Jeep ride in the beautiful red rocks. Then with a bittersweet feeling, we headed back home to Las Vegas.

For me, the most fun was flying to these amazing places. There is something therapeutic for me in flying. It is one of my passions. The fun we had as a family will be hard to match. If I could have given a lecture and played a round of golf, all my passions in life would have been combined in one trip.

I know most won't be able to do something like that, but if I were you, I would try to put together something that combines all of your passions. When I was a kid, my parents took us around the country in a station wagon. That's what life is all about. So, on the flying trip with my family, I was a kid again for three weeks. We all became less fearful by doing this trip. Make your life a daring adventure.

Security is superstition, it does not exist in nature
nor do the children of men as a whole experience it.
Avoiding danger is no safer in the long run
than outright exposure.
Life is either a daring adventure or nothing.
—HELEN KELLER,
American author, political activist, and lecturer

Many of my friends have conquered their fears of flying in a private plane by flying with me. One friend was scared to death to fly in a small plane. Let's call her Mary Jo. She told me that the only reason she would fly is because I was the pilot. For some reason she had an awesome sense of trust in me. But she conquered her fear. It must have been a serious fear because this woman courageously faced the evils of cancer head on. She has dealt with it every day for the past sixteen years. She's amazing and should write a book about dealing with cancer. I'm proud of anyone who can overcome their fears of flying with me because I know how afraid they were. Love and gratitude, Mary Jo.

Are your fears preventing you from enjoying life to the fullest? What are you missing?

- Have you missed seeing the colors of the deep blue sea because you're afraid to scuba dive or snorkel? There's an amazing world down there.

- Have you touched a big fish or a giant clam? Have you seen Nemo in the wild?

- Have you done something new that you always wanted to do? Have you seen sunset above the clouds, not below it?

- Have you ridden a horse in remote places in the world that you can only get to by small planes or kayak in the calm, tranquil, beautiful places of the world that you can only get to by a small plane or a float plane?

- Have you been scuba diving like James Bond with an underwater jet apparatus?

- Have you been deserted on a remote island with your significant other so you can have a romantic day in paradise?

- Have you kissed a dolphin?

- Have you seen the most beautiful places in the world?

My wife and I have done and seen all of those things and more. I encourage you to do the same. This is your one chance on this planet, don't waste it.

My mom and dad may have raised their kids to be opinionated, perhaps argumentative, and certainly competitive. Of course, that's my brother I'm talking about (big smile). And by example, my dad raised us to be honest. I can be brutally honest. I don't know how else to be. But they also raised their kids to be confident and passionate and loyal. They raised us to believe that we could do anything and to fear very little.

I never asked whether I was going to college; it was just a given in our family. Every time I did something, my parents would praise me and tell me what a great job I did, even if it was crap so I assumed I was good at it. So because of this constant positive feedback, I always thought I could do anything. They never discouraged me from trying new things. That gave me the freedom to try different things. Please don't instill fears in your children. Help them become all they can be like my parents did for me and my siblings.

> Defeat is not the worst of failures.
> Not to have tried is the true failure.
> **—GEORGE E. WOODBERRY,** American literary critic and poet

Successful people understand that failure is a natural part of making progress. Of course you're going to fail. We all fail sooner or later.

> One who fears failure limits his activities.
> Failure is only the opportunity to more intelligently begin again.
> **—HENRY FORD,** American business magnate

> The greatest test of courage on earth
> is to bear defeat without losing heart.
> **—ROBERT GREEN INGERSOLL,** American political leader

I paraphrase the line below from a movie called *Tuck Everlasting*: "Fear not failing to achieve your dreams; fear more the failure to even try." Can you imagine being on your deathbed and realizing that you never tried to achieve your dream? That would be far worse failing at your attempt.

> Greatness, in the last analysis, is largely due to bravery— courage in escaping from old ideas and old standards and respectable ways of doing things.
> —**JAMES HARVEY ROBINSON,** American historian

You need to eliminate irrational fears because success requires courage. And courage is contagious, even within yourself. The more irrational fears you can conquer, the more likely you'll conquer the fear of failing to achieve your dreams.

> To the daring belongs the future.
> —**EMMA GOLDMAN,** Canadian writer

Remember how I was scared to death to skydive. I wasn't absent of fear, I just conquered it.

> Courage is the resistance to fear, mastery of fear, not absence of fear.
> —**MARK TWAIN,** American humorist

I've shown you how to create the plan, now you just need the courage to do it. You can do nothing worthwhile without courage.

> Behold the turtle.
> He makes progress only when he sticks his neck out.
> —**JAMES B. CONANT,** president of Harvard University

No one should be ashamed or feel bad if they are afraid. Everyone has fears. It's not a crime to be afraid. It's not a weakness to be afraid. The problem is when you let fear win, when it prevents you from doing the things you need to or want to do.

Do not fear going forward slowly;
fear only to stand still.
—CHINESE PROVERB

Your courage will be tested by being a leader or being an innovator. Leadership makes you an easy target, so leading requires courage. Leadership won't give you courage, but courage will make you a leader. My mentor, Omer Reed, told me when I first started lecturing that when you're out in front, even your friends will mistake you for the enemy and you'll end up with arrows in your back. He was right, but it got to the point that there was no more room for any more arrows. I became numb to the arrows. It was as if they were hitting the other arrows that were already in my back. Don't let the arrows prevent you from carrying on toward your passion-driven purpose. As Ron Jackson told me, "Let your success be your answer." Love and gratitude, Omer and Ron!

I was told I was a fool to build the institute: "It'll never work, and the overhead will kill you. You're crazy." But they were wrong. I wouldn't be writing this book today if I hadn't taken that risk. The LVI campus is now 63,000 square feet on five acres. There is no private postgraduate school in the world like it.

Are you afraid to fail? My favorite quote of all time is from Theodore Roosevelt.

Far better is it to dare mighty things, to win glorious triumphs,
even though checkered by failure, than to take ranks with those
poor spirits who neither enjoy nor suffer much, because they live
in the gray twilight that knows not victory nor defeat.
—THEODORE ROOSEVELT, American president

There are too many people who live in that great twilight because they won't try anything. They're afraid of failure. But they never accomplish anything. I love that quote because it's poetic, profound, and beautifully written, but mostly because it's absolutely true.

So far we have learned to believe in a passion-driven purpose, to fuel that passion and stay positive while eliminating negativity and jealousy, and we've learned to conquer our fears. But do you have the will and desire to spend the energy necessary to achieve your dreams? Without desire, you won't be successful. In the next chapter, let's create the burning desire to achieve your dreams.

SUMMARY

- Make a list of your fears and determine if they are irrational.
- Conquer your irrational fears.
- Do things you are afraid to do.
- Challenge yourself.

Step Six

Master Your Desire and the Drive to Succeed

What we accomplish in life is based not on what we want but on how much we want it. A lack of desire can prevent people from succeeding. At LVI, we can't create successful dentists unless they want to be successful.

> You cannot push anyone up a ladder
> unless he's willing to climb a little himself.
> **—ANDREW CARNEGIE,** Scottish-American industrialist

As you define your goal or your vision or your dream, you need to ask yourself how much you really want it. How hard are you willing to work for it?

I would love to have a bodybuilder's body. Every year in the past, my New Year's resolution was to start working out and lifting weights. But I wasn't willing to work hard at it because I didn't want it that bad. I have a gorgeous wife who loves me even with this body of mine. I don't have the time, I would have to sacrifice something else to do it, and everything else is more important than that resolution.

If I had a magic wand and could instantly give myself that buff bod, I'd do it. But I don't want it enough to go to the gym every day. I never exercise. I know it's pathetic, but it's true. Don't get me wrong, I'm active, but I won't run a marathon and I don't lift weights. I'm not sure where I would find the time because I'm so busy with my passion-driven purpose.

So ask yourself if your dreams or goals are worth the effort. At the end of the day, was it really worth it to spend that much time and work that hard for it? To me it wouldn't be worth the effort to work out at the gym. I guess I'm not that vain. Maybe that's your passion. If so, then that's what you should do. I'm not judging, I'm just stating that it's not my passion. If it's yours, great, then be the best bodybuilder you can be.

Along the path toward your goals, you're going to run into obstacles. Obstacles are going to occur no matter what your goal is. They are part of life. Embrace the obstacles and learn something from them. Every difficulty is an opportunity to learn and grow. Life is not all sunshine, so welcome the rain.

> In the middle of every difficulty lies opportunity.
> **—ALBERT EINSTEIN**, theoretical physicist

You know the old saying, "What doesn't kill you makes you stronger." In many respects that's true. You have to have the burning desire to succeed to get past these obstacles. You may have to alter your plan. That's a given because rarely does one have smooth sailing all the way to their dreams.

> Difficulties mastered are opportunities won.
> **—WINSTON CHURCHILL**, British prime minister

Strong desire will create the action needed to achieve your goal. Results come from action, but most people usually just hope for success. Good results come from good actions. There is an old sailor's truth: "When the wind goes out of the sail, the boat drifts with the current."

Footprints in the sand of time
were not made by folks who stood still.
—UNKNOWN

Therefore, in order to implement the effort to fulfill your goal, you must be motivated. It's my job to motivate you; otherwise, you won't have the desire to achieve your goal. And then you won't be successful. There are three basic motivators.

- Money, but it is the weakest.

- Recognition and respect are strong.

- Purpose is the strongest.

Try not to become a man of success
but rather try to become a man of value.
—ALBERT EINSTEIN, theoretical physicist

So let's work on the strongest one, purpose. Can you make a difference in somebody's life? We've talked about that already and the answer is absolutely yes you can. Wouldn't that be a great purpose? Everyone has the power to make a difference and, in some way, change the life of someone else. One kind act may have a ripple effect that changes the world.

Your expectations determine actions. In the book *Talent Is Never Enough,* John Maxwell writes, "We cannot live in a way that is inconsistent with our expectations for ourselves."

We must be the change we wish to see in the world.
—GANDHI

Does the cat see a lion in the mirror? I have a very small dog, but she sees herself as a Great Dane. She barks at the big dogs like she can whip their behind. How do you see yourself? Do you think you make a difference?

Do you think you have no impact on anyone? Even small actions can have an impact.

> No individual raindrop ever considered itself
> responsible for the flood.
> **—UNKNOWN**

Leadership

Going from good to great requires leadership. Why? Because you need to lead your team toward your goals. You may be motivated, but you need to motivate your team. What makes a good leader?

In the book *Launching a Leadership Revolution,* Chris Brady and Orrin Woodward wrote about the characteristics of a leader:

- Dissatisfaction

- Perpetual student, teachable

- Character

Let's talk about dissatisfaction. It might seem weird that the authors would say that leaders need to be dissatisfied. But it's true. To go from good to great, leaders need to be discontented with the status quo. Comfort kills ambition and creates complacency. That can stop progress toward your vision. If you are satisfied, your drive to work on becoming great is eliminated.

Dissatisfaction is correlated with a desire to do more. Why is it enough for you to just be good? Why do some people say, "Well I don't care to become great?" Why is there no desire to be better? What is the difference between the great and the mediocre? Is being good the enemy of being great? The answer is yes!

When you are good, you can become complacent. You become satisfied and comfortable. Maybe it's because you are making a good living, but comfort provides no motivation to do better. So search your soul and decide if you are motivated to do more. Are you willing to make a 100 percent effort?

Perhaps you are wondering why comfort is a bad thing. One of the problems I have is getting dentists to listen to the amazing changes in dentistry at LVI. That's because they are comfortable. They don't want to step out of their comfort zone. They feel safe. The president of a major dental company that sells EMG equipment (we'll call him Greg) said to me, "You know what your job is and what you're so good at." He continued. "Your job is to make people uncomfortable. That's what you're good at."

I never thought about that before, but he's right. I realize that I make people very uncomfortable. It's hard to get insecure people to listen. They don't like feeling uncomfortable. They want to think they know every-thing. It's why they pick lectures that tell them what they already know. But leaders want to be uncomfortable, to know things they don't know, to stretch their boundaries.

Insecurity is also why people criticize those who make them feel uncomfortable. It takes a strong person to admit that they might be wrong and that they need to know more. Secure people cherish those who make them feel uncomfortable because they know they are moving from good to great.

Stretch your paradigms to new limits. It will make you master your passion-driven purpose—at least until the next uncomfortable feeling comes along. Embrace the feeling of discomfort. As the saying goes, good enough seldom is. Don't settle for just good. Good is the enemy of great.

Maybe you are content with mediocrity because financially you're doing well. Do you not want to just become better at whatever you do regardless of the financial impact? Do you say, "I don't need to do that because I'm making all this money"? Does that make you proud of what you have accomplished or provided? Do you just want to be wealthy or do you want to be one of the best? Can you live with yourself knowing that your customer would be better off with someone else or some-where else?

Let's say you don't care if you're really good. What about what's best for your clients or customers? Are you preventing yourself from becoming great because you're settling? Most people want comfort and will not step out of their comfort zone to seek excellence. And in my opinion, that's sad. You're wasting your potential.

The worst thing that can happen in your quest for your vision is that you become satisfied.

Resist Frustration

You need to remain dissatisfied, but only to a point. Being discontented can lead to frustration. And frustration can affect your attitude. If you become discouraged, it's over. So you need to remain discontented, but you have to resist frustration.

I've seen it many times. Somebody got frustrated and they quit, instead of finding solutions to end the frustration. You must remain focused on your vision and the path to get there. Do all you can to resist frustration.

Leading a Team

You may have the desire to achieve your goals, but does your team? To achieve your passion-filled purpose, most of you will need a team! And they need you to lead them. Few people have achieved success without a team. So how do you lead your team? To create success, you need to be a great leader. To be a great leader you need to create desire in your team.

Teamwork is the ability to work together
toward a common vision, the ability to direct
individual accomplishments toward organizational objectives.
It is the fuel that allows common people
to attain uncommon results.
—ANDREW CARNEGIE, Scottish-American industrialist

All we can ever do in a way of good to people
is to encourage them to do good to themselves.
—RANDOLPH BOURNE, American writer

Leadership means you must be a hands-on leader. You can't delegate your leadership.

If your vision is for a year, plant wheat.
If your vision is for ten years, plant trees.
If your vision is for a lifetime, plant people.
—CHINESE PROVERB

At LVI we plant people to help us in our purpose. We've planted thousands of people through our education process. But hiring people to work for us hasn't been as easy. People are like icebergs; there is much more to them than meets the eye. So don't give up on people. Some are like diamonds, they just need more polishing. Judging people is tough. I've failed in this many times. It's one of my weaknesses. I'm not a good judge of character. People I thought were good turned out to be the opposite. People I've made wealthy turned out not to deserve my efforts. Some people I was leery of turned out to be fantastic. This is something I can't help you with. I wish I could, but I find it hard to recognize a wolf in sheep's clothing.

There is something that is much scarcer,
something finer far, something rarer than ability.
It is the ability to recognize ability.
—ELBERT HUBBARD, American writer

Who's on your team? Are they the right people? Did you hire a who or a what? What do I mean by that? Did you hire a person who does a particular job? That's a what. Like an office manager.

Or did you hire a who? Did you hire somebody who has great people skills, who has great attitude, who has a great personality? That's a who. If not, that's who you need to hire. Don't hire whats, hire whos. So how many who's are on your team?

I love this commercial as this guy talks to his team during a team meeting:

The Boss: Okay. The presentation is tomorrow so let's make sure we all know our usual responsibilities. Jeff, you keep feeding the old information. Dean, I need you to continue not living up to your resume. Sue, you're in charge of waffling.

Sue: Are you sure?

The Boss: Jerome, you'll talk a big game then do nothing.

Jerome: Let's do it.

The Boss: Rick, can you fold under pressure for me?

Rick: Like a lawn chair.

The Boss: And Ted, you just keep thinking everyone is out to get you.

Ted: They are?

The Boss: I'll be at FedEx Kinkos where they'll help me design, print, copy, and finish the proposal.

If that's the type of person you have on your team, get them off the bus and get the right people on the bus. If they are a who, you can mold them into a what—to achieve your passion-driven purpose.

If I accept you as you are I will make you worse;
however, if I treat you as though you are what you are
capable of becoming, I help you become that.
—JOHANN WOLFGANG VON GOETHE, writer

Don't give up on people too soon. It may be your fault that they're not living up to your expectations. Remember that when leading a team gets tough, people may quit on a business, but they usually won't quit on a friend. Do your team members love their jobs? Do the people around you enjoy your path toward your goals? Are you projecting hope?

> A leader is a dealer in hope.
> **—NAPOLEON BONAPARTE,**
> French statesman and military leader

Don't ever give up and say, "Well, we're not going to do well this year because of the economy." That's not hope. You have to be a dealer in hope. There is nothing more important than hope.

Most People Are Motivated

I believe that most people are motivated. When you hire people, they are usually motivated. The problem is that most leaders demotivate the team by not giving them recognition and encouragement when they do well. Everyone needs to feel appreciated and needed.

I admit that I had a hard time complimenting my team. I thought that excellence should be everyone's goal. It took me years to realize that not everyone is as driven as I am. Some say crazy!

To help me compliment my team more often, I did the dime trick. I would put ten dimes in my right pocket. Each time I complimented a person, I would move a dime from my right pocket to the left pocket. When I got all ten in my left pocket, I could take them out. That was a relief, because I don't like coins clanging around in my pants.

With my right pocket loaded with dimes, I would walk around the office looking for things that someone was doing well so I could compliment them. Generally, all my dimes were gone by lunch, which is why everybody thought I was tired or grumpy in the afternoon.

The point is this: Don't drag, lead. It's very difficult to drag a reluctant team along with you. You have to create the desire in your team to be a leader.

One last thing about leadership: It requires you to be proactive. Being a leader means standing up for what you believe is right. Don't let bad things go unanswered. If you see wrong, right it! If you see evil, confront it!

> The only thing necessary for the triumph of evil
> is for good men to do nothing.
> **—EDMUND BURKE,**
> Irish statesman, author, orator, political theorist and philosopher

Now that you have determined if you have the desire and leadership to accomplish your passion-driven purpose, you need to be aware of one thing that will stop you from achieving your goal. And that's not quitting. Let's move to the next step—perseverance.

SUMMARY

- Get the right people on your bus.
- Get the wrong ones off.
- Work on your leadership.
- Motivate others.

STEP SEVEN
Persevere

You've created the desire. Now, at what point do you quit? When do you realize that your goal or dream is not going to happen? Most people give up too soon. If you are going to be successful, you need to persevere.

Consider the three necessary Ps to success along with the three Es I mentioned early.

Passion, Purpose, and Perseverance

> Many of life's failures are people who did not realize how close they were to success when they gave up.
> **—THOMAS EDISON,** American inventor

Assuming that you have the desire to be great, are you giving up too soon? Are you making excuses for not trying? Are you making excuses for failing?

Let me give you typical excuses:

- We can't do that here.

- I don't have those kinds of clients.

- It's the economy.

- It's my team's fault.

- It's my family's fault.

> Ninety-nine percent of failure
> comes from people who have a habit
> of making excuses.
> **—GEORGE WASHINGTON CARVER,**
> American botanist and inventor

An excuse puts blame on something or someone other than you—the economy, location, the town, whatever. Excuses give you permission to fail. You take the control away from yourself when you say, "It's not my fault." If it's not your fault and therefore outside your control, then there is nothing you can do about it. And that's what you do—nothing!

The problem occurs when you give yourself an excuse. You've eliminated the possibility of success because you stop trying. You stop trying because it's not your fault and there is nothing you can do to change it. To make an excuse means you're giving up. You know the old saying about excuses—they are like anal sphincters, we all have one and they all stink. No more excuses.

I see many people blame their failures on everyone else. Ego and pride get in the way, and bad decisions continue. They fail because they won't listen to the unpleasant truths and accept responsibility.

> If you could kick the person in the pants
> responsible for most of your trouble,
> you wouldn't sit for a month.
> **—THEODORE ROOSEVELT,** American president

People with the weakest character tend to place blame on their circumstances. They become victims. Circumstances may be beyond your control, but your character is not. Again, everything you do in life is your choice. How you conduct yourself, how you treat others, your attitude, your honesty. And there are consequences to choices we make. Bad choices usually have bad ramifications.

Hold yourself responsible for a higher standard
than anyone else expects of you.
—HENRY WARD BEECHER,
American clergyman and abolitionist

Never Give Up

Never give up, for that is just the place
and time that the tide will turn.
—HARRIET BEECHER STOWE, American abolitionist and author

In the movie *Martian Child,* the kid, Dennis, was adopted by a man played by John Cusack. The kid kept claiming he was a Martian, so he would wear little weights on his ankles to hold him down so gravity didn't pull him up. The authorities were thinking about taking the child away from John Cusack because he wouldn't face reality.

So the dad told the boy that the authorities were going to talk to him and that he should tell them about all of the human stuff they like to do.

Dennis agreed to that request. Then he asked if he could tell them he was a Martian.

His dad reluctantly said no because the authorities might take Dennis away.

The man interviewing Dennis asked him how he was getting along at school and if there was something he wanted to tell them?

Dennis said no.

Then the lady interviewing him asked him if all this moving from school to school had been hard for him?

And then Dennis repeated my favorite line (paraphrase): "Mmm, there's been some rough times, but the important thing is to, um, you have to face your problems and you should never ever, ever, ever, ever give up. Never ever, ever, ever. Winston Churchill said that. I think."

The male interviewer smiled and told him that Winston Churchill was a very smart man.

So the dad (Cusack) got to keep him because of that comment: "Never ever, ever give up." Look at Walt Disney who was rejected 301 times for a loan until finally getting a yes. What has he done with that? Wouldn't that be horrible if he didn't persevere? What would have happened if there was no "happiest place on earth"?

- It is said that Abraham Lincoln lost seventeen elections before he won one. Wouldn't it be terrible if he had given up?

- Stephen King's first novel, *Carrie,* was rejected thirty times before it was published.

- Henry Ford failed two times before in ventures that abruptly resulted in bankruptcies, prior to successfully launching the Ford Motor Company.

- Bill Gates failed in his first business attempt.

- Colonel Sanders was sixty-two when he took a $105 social security check in hand to pitch his chicken recipe to restaurants, after 1,009 folks told him he was crazy, but he didn't give up.

- Sir James Dyson had 5,126 failures before he finally got his vacuum right.

- Thomas Edison failed over ten thousand times to invent a commercially viable electric lightbulb, but he didn't give up. He was asked if he felt like a failure after failing nine thousand times, and Edison simply stated, "Why would I feel like a failure? And why would I ever give up? I now know definitely over nine thousand ways an electric lightbulb will not work. Success is almost in my grasp."

Nothing in the world can take the place of persistence.
Talent will not. Nothing is more common than unsuccessful men
with talent. Genius will not; unrewarded genius is almost a proverb.
Education will not; the world is full of educated derelicts.
Persistence and determination alone are omnipotent.
—CALVIN COOLIDGE, American president

In the book *The Dip*, Seth Godin writes about a trait that occurs in any endeavor. He describes the dip. The dip is the long slog between starting and mastering. Almost everything in life worth doing is affected by the dip. The dip is the tough part and that's when most people give up.

We all have started a new thing. Maybe you wanted to snowboard. When you first started, it was great. You immediately got the rush of the quick, easy way. And then you hit the dip. Progress becomes very hard, requiring a lot of work and perseverance.

But the dip is good. It creates value for your achievement. If it wasn't for the dip, there would be many people doing it. Scarcity is what makes it valuable. It's easy to be a CEO; what's difficult is getting there. There is a huge dip along the way.

"Successful people don't just ride out the dip," Godin says in his book. "They don't, they just don't buckle down and survive it; no, they lean into the dip."

They push harder, changing the rules as they go. Just because you know you're in the dip doesn't mean you have to be happy with it. Dips don't last quite as long when you work hard. When you hit a brick wall, chip away at that brick and you'll get through it.

> It does not matter how slowly you go
> as long as you do not stop.
> **—CONFUCIUS**

Speaking of flying, did the Wright brothers ever quit? No. Did Charles Lindbergh ever quit? No. Did Chuck Yeager ever quit? No. Did Neil Armstrong ever quit? No. Did Theodore Smith ever quit?

Wait, you don't know who Theodore Smith is? Of course, you've never heard of him—because he quit!

> Every successful person finds that great success lies just beyond
> the point when they're convinced their idea is not going to work.
> **—NAPOLEON HILL,** American self-help author

The reason a football game is decided after four quarters is because of the importance of endurance. Those in better shape will eventually win. A PGA match lasts four days because it's the great golfers who can keep up the focus for four rounds. It's not unusual that the person who was leading on the first day doesn't win the tournament. The winner perseveres.

> You can't get much done in life
> if you only work on the days you feel good.
> **—JERRY WEST**

Do you give up and start something else or do you keep working at it? What have you given up on lately? Did you really try as hard and persevere as long as you could? From now on, never stop! You may be closer than you think.

There is the story of the three men walking through the desert. The first one comes up to an abandoned well. He begins to pump the well. He pumps and pumps and pumps. No water comes out, so he continues to walk and dies of dehydration. The second man does the same. He pumps and pumps and pumps and nothing comes out, so he quits and continues to walk through the desert and also dies of dehydration. The third man gets to the well, but he doesn't give up. He continues to pump until eventually the pump becomes primed and water comes pouring out. The third man rehydrated himself and made it out of the desert alive.

What the others couldn't see was the water was almost to the top of the pipe, but they gave up before it got to the top and primed the pump.

You may have heard the story of 212. It's about 212 degrees. That's the boiling temperature of water. At 211 degrees it's just hot water. It's basically worthless. At 212 degrees water boils and becomes steam and that steam can power a locomotive. One little degree makes all the difference in the world. A silly degree!

So make your water boil. Just turn it up a little bit. Just give it a harder try. Persevere just a little longer. Hang on just a bit more. You may be at 211 degrees with where you are in launching your vision, so give that little extra to drive your passion.

Maybe you heard the parable of the donkey in the well. Yes, another well story. One day a farmer's donkey fell into a well. The animal cried piteously for hours as the farmer tried to figure out what to do. Finally, he decided the animal was old and the well needed to be covered up anyway, so it just wasn't worth it to retrieve the donkey. He invited all his neighbors to come over and help him. They all grabbed a shovel and began shoveling dirt into the well.

At first the donkey realized what was happening and cried horribly. Then to everyone's amazement he quieted down. A few shovel loads later, the farmer finally looked down the well. He was astonished at what he saw. With each shovel of dirt that hit his back, the donkey was doing something amazing. He would shake it off and take a step up. As the farmer's neighbors continued to shovel dirt on top of the animal, he would shake it off and take a step up. Pretty soon everyone was amazed as the donkey stepped up over the edge of the well and happily trotted off.

> The most important thing in life is not to capitalize on our gains.
> Any fool can do that. The really important thing
> is to profit from our losses. That requires intelligence;
> it makes the difference between a man of sense and a fool.
> **—WILLIAM BOLITHO,** South African journalist

Life is going to shovel dirt on you, all kinds of dirt. The trick to getting out of the well is to shake it off and take a step up. Each of your troubles is a stepping-stone. We can get out of the deepest wells by not stopping, never giving up, shaking off the dirt, and taking a step up.

> The greater the obstacle the more the glory in overcoming it.
> **—MOLIERE,** French playwright

The story goes that donkey later came back and bit the farmer who had tried to bury him. The bite got infected and the farmer eventually died in agony from septic shock. The moral of that lesson? When you do something wrong and try to cover your ass, it's always going to come back to bite you.

EXERCISE
What Are the Adversities in Your Life
Write down the top five adversities you had to face. Yes, another list. Now, put down next to each adversity one of the following terms that fits:

- Failure
- Avoidance
- Success

Now, score how you did. It will tell you who you are. Did you have more successes than failures? How many adversities did you avoid? Obviously you want more victories than avoidance or failures. If you have fewer successes it doesn't mean you have to stay that way; it just shows you the changes that need to be made.

> Don't let yesterday take up too much of today.
> If you focus on today instead of yesterday
> you'll have a better tomorrow.
> **—WILL ROGERS,** American writer and humorist

To persevere, you must be willing to change and be willing to adapt to change. Many people have trouble adapting to change, yet change is always going to happen. You can't avoid it if you want to succeed in life. Many people never solve their problems because they refuse to change.

> We should not look back unless it's to derive useful lessons from past errors, and for the purpose of profiting by dearly bought experience.
> **—GEORGE WASHINGTON,** first president of the US

Let's say you are determined to not give up. To succeed you need to be open to new ideas and to change—let's look at the importance of being teachable in the next chapter.

SUMMARY

- Learn from past mistakes where you quit.
- Decide that you won't give up in the future.
- Give it that little extra on your current plan.

Step Eight
Be Teachable

One of the saddest things I've discovered in my career of trying to educate professionals is that they get to a point where they think they know it all and stop learning. But they need to know that they don't know what they don't know. You can't know what you can't see, and if you are not trained to "see" certain things, then you will miss out on advancement in your chosen path. Also, what you think is the best may not be.

Are you teachable? If you think too highly of your talent, then you may not be teachable.

> I am the wisest man alive, for I know one thing,
> and that is that I know nothing.
> **—SOCRATES**, Greek philosopher

Do you regularly read books? How many other books have you read? These statistics, from *a 2003 survey conducted by a company called The Jenkins Group*, is shocking:

- 58 percent of the US population never reads another book after high school.
- 42 percent of college grads never read another book.

- 80 percent of US families did not buy or read a book last year.

- 70 percent of US adults have not been in a bookstore in the last five years.

- 57 percent of new books are not read to completion. In fact, most readers do not get past page eighteen in a book. Please finish this one!

> The education of a man is never completed until he dies.
> **—ROBERT E. LEE,** commander of the Confederate States army

Become a perpetual student, having an open mind, a thirst for knowledge, a passion for excellence, and the desire to be your best.

Being teachable leads to success. Successful people view learning differently from those who are unsuccessful.

> Education is the kindling of a flame,
> not the filling of a vessel.
> **—SOCRATES,** Greek philosopher

Talented people are the toughest to teach. One of the most frustrating things with my job at LVI is having to deal with those who don't think they can learn anything more. They are talented, but that doesn't mean they can't be better. Don't let your talent get in the way of your success. Be teachable.

> Do you see a man who is wise in his own eyes?
> There is more hope for a fool than for him.
> **—PROVERB**

Leonardo da Vinci's list of accomplishments was amazing. Here is what he did in his life.

- Sculptor

- Painter

- Anatomy expert

- Hydraulic expert

- Optics expert

- Designed buildings

- Engineered fortifications

- Manufactured heavy equipment

- Athlete

- Musician

- Singer

- Mathematician

- Predicted submarines, helicopters, and other modern inventions before they even had the capability or materials to make them.

Bill Gates believes that Leonardo da Vinci was the most amazing person to ever live, and I agree with that. What made da Vinci was not his talents or his ability, it was his teachability. So look within. Are you teachable?

If you think you know everything, that you're always right and others are wrong, then ask yourself how you know that? Again, you don't know what you don't know. If you knew it, you would know it! Perhaps you don't see yourself as others do. Ask someone you trust where they think you need to grow. Don't be defensive in this exercise. The more actions that require courage, the braver you become. Success is due to the discipline of investing in yourself with knowledge. In order to be successful, you must prepare the best you can through learning and practice.

> If I had eight hours to chop down a tree
> I'd spend six sharpening my axe.
> **—ABRAHAM LINCOLN,** American president

Learning never stops. Take your game to the next level. Find someone to help you. I have flying mentors. I told this dentist one time that I was going flying with an instructor, and he asked, "Why do you need to continue learning to fly? Don't you know how?"

I said, "Why do you go to continuing education courses? Don't you know how to do dentistry?"

> Men give me credit for genius.
> All the genius I have lies in this;
> when I have a subject in hand I study it profoundly.
> **—ALEXANDER HAMILTON,**
> founding father of the US

I read flying publications, I do online courses, I take seminars in flying. I have a simulator at home so if I'm not flying for a while I can play with it. I prepare before each flight. I have a checklist I go through before, during, and after each flight.

> Luck is what happens when
> preparation meets opportunity.
> **—SENECA,** Roman philosopher

Ongoing learning is also important because we can forget what we learned. Learning also helps us to weed out bad information.

> What we do on some great occasion
> will probably depend on what we already are.
> And what we are will be the result of
> previous years of self-discipline.
> **—HENRY PARRY LIDDON,** English theologian

If you develop a thirst for knowledge, the world opens up to you. If you knew you were going to die tomorrow, you would go out today and live the fullest day of your life. But if you knew that you were going to live forever, you would want to learn everything about everything.

> Live as if you were to die tomorrow.
> Learn as if you were to live forever.
> **—GANDHI**

I think you should live life to your fullest, but be a master at something. Maybe as many things as you can. Don't be the fool on the playground. Try to get a basic understanding of as much as you can and then master the things you're passionate about. If you're teachable, you have limitless potential, and with limitless potential you can achieve greatness.

So what are the roadblocks to becoming teachable?

Arrogance

Arrogance produces ignorance, and there's lots of arrogance out there. It closes the mind. Humility opens the door to learning. I try now to have an open mind about everything.

> Nothing is more securely lodged
> in the ignorance of the experts.
> **—F. A. HAYEK,** Austrian-British economist

So you think you're a bigshot. Some of you are saying, "Yeah I'm really good. I'm the best in my community." Maybe you're known in your town. Maybe you're known in your state. Maybe you're even nationally known. Maybe you're even internationally known. You've accomplished a lot on this planet.

But compare the earth to the rest of the planets. Look how big Jupiter is compared to Earth. Look how big our sun is compared to the Earth and Jupiter.

Look how big the other suns out there are to our sun. You're a speck on a speck.

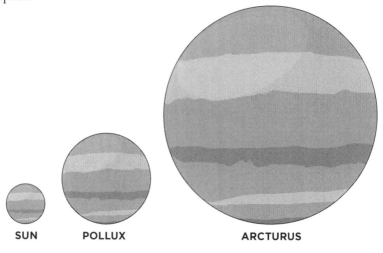

But it gets worse. If you look at Arcturus and compare it to Antares, you can see Arcturus is a little tiny thing.

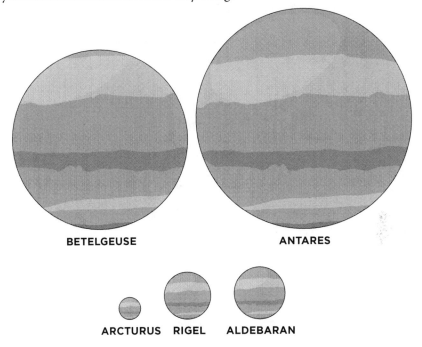

BETELGEUSE   ANTARES

ARCTURUS   RIGEL   ALDEBARAN

I encourage you to find on the Internet where you can see Hubble telescope views of entire galaxies billions of light-years away that are bigger than ours. Sombrero galaxy, twenty-eight million light-years from Earth, is fifty thousand light-years across, meaning that it would take fifty-thousand years for light to reach the other side. That ought to humble you.

Unless you're president or someone important like that, nobody will remember you in a hundred years. So do the best you can now, but don't do anything for that reason. Don't get me wrong, you can make a difference in our little world, but do it for the right reason. Try to change the world for the better. Make life better for those around you. Be an example of what you want the world to be. Try to leave it in a better state than when you came into it.

Some people ask me, "What does it matter what I do? A hundred years from now, my life will have made no difference." Although I understand the question, it's pessimistic. You don't know if your small contribution will make a difference. We've all heard of the butterfly effect, where the flapping of the wings of a butterfly in the Amazon rainforest can cause a tornado in Texas two weeks later. Wouldn't you be happier leaving our world knowing that you made a difference rather than just existing?

> No snowflake in an avalanche ever feels responsible.
> **—VOLTAIRE,** French enlightenment writer,
> historian, and philosopher

How do you know if you're arrogant? There is a difference between being confident and being arrogant. I want you to be confident. Knowledge is thrown at you all the time, but when you're arrogant you can't receive that knowledge; it doesn't hit you unless it hits you square on the head for some reason.

When you're arrogant, you are not teachable. Instead, humble yourself and gather information with an open mind, and in no time you will become more knowledgeable.

> Arrogance is a roadblock on the highway of wisdom.
> **—AMERICAN PROVERB**

My profession is loaded with arrogant people, even people we taught at LVI. They think that since they learned from us once, that there is nothing else they can learn from us. What they don't understand is that we've never stopped learning. We have evolved and advanced. Every year we become more knowledgeable, and we spread that knowledge to those who are willing to listen. We continue to research and discover so that we can share that information with those wanting to be their best.

As you gain more information, your mental bucket becomes full. So you need to drain out bad information that prevents you from learning new things. You have to wipe the chalkboard clean to make room for new information. Don't assume that what you think is a fact will always be accurate. I believe what has kept LVI going so long and so successfully is that, unlike other educational places, we never assumed that we had all the answers. We continued to grow and evolve. As I say in my lectures, if you quote me, date me. Because I may not believe or say the same thing a year from now.

Habits

Habits are another reason people aren't teachable: "We've always done it this way; that's how everyone does it." If you get stuck thinking that the way you were taught is the only way it can be done, you will fall behind as others race by you. When someone tells me that a method was developed by the founding member of an organization thirty years ago, I know that the place is doomed to fail. If the founder was still alive today, he or she would probably be evolving. Don't let habits prevent you from discovering better ways and ideas.

> A long habit of not thinking a thing wrong
> gives it a superficial appearance of being right.
> **—THOMAS PAINE,** founding father of the US

Ego

A lot of "experts" won't take on something because they didn't think of it. Or that's not the way they were taught. Ego closes our minds to new ideas. Ego is the number one hindrance to teachability, which prevents us from admitting our mistakes and prevents us from making needed changes. So many prevent themselves from becoming better because they believe they are at the top or don't want others to think they aren't experts. The side of the road to success is littered with those who thought they had already arrived.

We once had a faculty member at LVI who would never adopt anything that he didn't think of. Perhaps arrogance prevented him from adopting new ideas, because he believed he was the expert. Or perhaps his problem was ego, meaning that he didn't want to admit that he didn't know something, or that someone was smarter than him. Sadly he refused to learn from others. And even more sadly he's now way behind in the knowledge necessary to help people. This is true of many "experts" and why they become "has-beens"!

> Pride is tasteless, colorless and size-less,
> yet it is the hardest thing to swallow.
> **—UNKNOWN**

No matter how awesome you think you are, don't take yourself so seriously. Realize that you may be someone now but not in the future. So learn to be self-deprecating. Learn to laugh at yourself. We all have weaknesses, and it's OK! And for your own sake, be a kid forever.

> Blessed are they that laugh at themselves
> for they shall never cease to be entertained.
> **—CHINESE PROVERB**

> Do not take life too seriously.
> You will never get out of it alive.
> **—ELBERT HUBBARD,** American writer

Losing Focus

Often life will prevent us from accomplishing important things. You end up managing details rather than leading your team toward your vision. As Godin wrote in *The Dip,* all our successes are the same, all our failures too. We fail when we get distracted by tasks we could delegate. We all get distracted by daily "things." Our mission drifts because mundane and urgent things take away our focus. It would be helpful to have someone who can help you with those things that prevent you from accomplishing your passion-driven purpose.

Concentrate all your thoughts upon the work at hand.
The sun's rays do not burn until brought to a focus.
—ALEXANDER GRAHAM BELL, American inventor

Character

Unless you are teachable, character is hampered by ignorance. People can say anything they like, but it's their actions that demonstrate the truth. I've learned that people will tell you one thing and then do something different. Their actions speak louder than their words. Do you lie to protect your mistakes? Do you omit important information that might shed a bad light on you? Do you take responsibility for your actions? Are you a decent and honest person?

Character cannot be developed in ease and quiet.
Only through experience of trial and suffering
can the soul be strengthened, vision cleared,
ambition inspired, and success achieved.
—HELEN KELLER,
American author, political activist, and lecturer

It's important to be real and clearly express yourself. Let people know what you're doing and thinking. They may not like you, but they will always know where you stand and will respect you. They will trust you.

Reason often makes mistakes, but conscience never does.
—JOSH BILLINGS, American humorist

Someone once compared me to a person who was jealous of my success. She said, "They may not like you because you can be brutally honest, but they always know where you stand, and they respect you for that. They may like him, but they also know he's a snake in the grass, and they don't respect him."

In matter of styles swim with the current;
in matter of principles stand like a rock.
—**THOMAS JEFFERSON**, Americn president

You'll find character in this amazing news story from ESPN.

It wasn't a famous game, or even a professional sport. It was in a small town in the middle of Washington State. There were fewer than one hundred people watching the game. It was a women's softball game. It was the second game of a softball doubleheader between Central Washington and Western Oregon.

It was an important game nonetheless. It was the college championship game. As a senior, this was Sarah Tucholsky's last chance to win a championship. She'd never hit a home run before, not in college, not in her life. At 5-feet-2-inches she was not a homerun power hitter.

Yet here she was with two runners on base. She connected on the hit of her life. She said she just wanted to hit it, and hit it she did. The ball sailed over the fence for a home run. Everyone was cheering and those on base were jumping up and down as they ran the bases. In her excitement, Sara missed touching first base as she rounded it and started toward second base. She quickly stopped and turned back to make sure she touched the base.

Her leg gave out as she pivoted, and she fell to the ground. Sarah was in a lot of pain. She had torn her ACL. It was a freak accident at the most inopportune time.

Sarah crawled back to first base and realized she couldn't make it around the bases to complete the only home run she would hit in her life. When she got back to first base, she just laid there and hugged the base. The coach went up to the umpire and asked what the ruling would be if they put in someone for Sarah. The umpire informed the coach that it would be a two-run single. When asked if anybody on her team could help Sarah get around the bases, the umpire would have to call her out. So no one on her team could touch her.

That's when the opposing team, Central Washington, did something with character like few have ever seen. Mallory Holtman, a player with more homeruns than any other in conference history, went to the home umpire and asked if she could pick her up and carry her around the bases. The umpire said, "Yes you can do that."

So Mallory walked up to Sarah and asked her, "Is it okay if we pick you up and carry you around the bases?" Sarah said, "Yes, and thank you." Mallory said, "You hit the ball over the fence, you deserve it."

So because she deserved it, Holtman and another player named Liz Wallace began to carry Sarah around the bases, stopping to touch her left foot on each base as they rounded the bases working their way to the home base to complete the homerun. All three started laughing because they wondered what this would look like to all the people in the stands.

Sarah said, "When I looked up I didn't see, you know, giant like smiles and screams. I saw emotion and tears and people crying."

It was a great example of character. The coaches were emotional, the players had tears in their eyes, the people in the stands were over-whelmed with pride, for they were watching the first home run by someone playing her last game of her college career and she was being carried by the opposing team to make it a reality.

Let's bring the character of that example even more to light. Central Washington lost the game that day 4-2. But they won more than they lost. They set an example of what character is all about. And what does Sarah think about Mallory? She said, "I have a lot of respect for her and put her in high regards, her and her teammates and I can't thank her enough."

> Talent can be cultivated in tranquillity;
> character only in the rushing stream of life.
> **—GOETHE,** German writer and statesman

Western Oregon went on to win its first conference championship in softball in school history. And even though the three ladies will be linked forever by that homerun, Sarah, Mallory, and Liz share something else in common. They are academic first team in the great Northwest Athletic Conference.

You see there are four kinds of people in this world.

- One who does the right thing without being told.

- One who does the right thing when told.

- One who does the right thing when told more than once.

- One who never does the right thing.

Those girls did the right thing. What kind of person are you?

> It's easy to dodge our responsibilities
> but we cannot dodge the consequences
> of dodging our responsibilities.
> **—JOSEPH STAMP,** English industrialist

Do you walk the talk? Are you providing the best service for your customers, your family, your friends? Let's make sure you are in the next chapter.

SUMMARY

- Accept responsibility for your actions.
- Remove any arrogance you have.
- Have an open mind.
- Be of strong character.

Step Nine
Serve Others

Anyone in business needs to understand this truth: Your customers are your boss. Your business is like golf. If you fail to understand and master the basics of the game, you will usually not do well. Their perception of you is their reality and good service is key to a good perception of you. If that's not there, chances are you'll be fired.

> There's only one boss, the customer,
> and he or she can fire anybody in the company
> from the chairman on down simply by
> spending his money somewhere else.
> **—SAM WALTON,** American businessman and entrepreneur

No matter what you do, you need to do your best, give it your all, and try to please the customer. If you're a stay-at-home mom, be the best stay-at-home mom you can be. If you are a delivery person, give them the best service you can with a happy positive attitude.

> Whatever you are, be a good one.
> **—ABRAHAM LINCOLN,** American president

Can you make a difference? In *The Simple Truth of Service,* Ken Blandford writes about Johnny the bagger who had Down Syndrome. Everyday Johnny would write a bunch of thoughts for the day and he would give them out to his customers. The lines where he bagged groceries were three times longer than lines at any other cash register. People would shop at that store just because of Johnny, just to get his thought for the day.

> It's little things that make the big things possible,
> only close attention to the fine details of any operation
> makes the operation first class.
> **—J. WILLARD MARRIOTT,** American entrepreneur and businessman

Pay attention to the detail. In a Lexus car commercial, a marble rolls around all the details of the car like something Rube Goldberg would create. It was the most expensive car commercial ever made. What if you paid that much attention to the detail of the way things worked at your office? Can you do better? We can always do better.

> The biggest room in the world
> is the room for improvement.
> **—CHINESE PROVERB**

Rocco

Speaking of Lexus, here's a true story that profoundly affected my life. When I was younger, I drove what I call a poor man's sports car, a Pontiac Fiero. It was not a good car and constantly in the shop. Dealing with the local dealership was like going to the DMV—painful. The service department acted as if they were doing me a favor by fixing my car. I would have to wait for a long time before someone would even acknowledge that I was around, even though I was standing next to my car waiting for service.

I got rid of that car and bought a Mazda RX7. That was a great car and it was cool to drive. But my first son was born, and we needed a four door to easily get the baby car seat in and out of the back seat. I heard good things about the Lexus from a friend. I ended up getting one of the less expensive models from a salesman named Rocco. That was the last time I ever saw the dealership for the next twenty-six years.

No, it's not what you think. During those twenty-six years I bought at least six new cars from Rocco. Most of them were the big SUVs because I needed to transport my kids and their friends around. When my two oldest boys were either out of college or in college, I decided to downsize to the Lexus Hybrid RX, just to be as green as I could.

Lexus makes great cars. But I was a loyal Lexus customer because of the service. Truth is, I could have received pretty much the same care from Toyota for many thousands less. So why didn't I do that? I stayed with Lexus because Rocco was the epitome of customer service for any industry.

Anytime my car needed to be serviced, Rocco would pick it up at my work. He would either leave me a loaner or bring it back the same day. Understand that between my work schedule, travel schedule, kids' school and activities schedule, I was a very busy man. The fact that I never had to cope with my old dealership's gruff customer service was a huge benefit to me.

I told you that I went through many Lexus cars over those twenty-six years. How did I escape having to go into the Lexus dealership? When it was time for a new car, or my lease was up, or Rocco thought I would love some new features in the new cars, he would bring them to my work and let me test drive them. If I wanted to see another color, he would bring that car to me. If I decided to get the car, he would take my old one in and get the new one fixed up, bring the paperwork back, and complete the transaction at my location.

Wait, there's more! During those twenty-six years, I never went into the DMV to register a car. Rocco would do that for me. This was before they had online registrations. I would go to work in the morning and get in a new car that afternoon. When the new plates came in, Rocco would bring them over and put them on for me. So for twenty-six years, I never saw the Lexus dealership and I never had to stand in line at the DMV, except for when I took my boys to get their driver's licenses.

There was only one reason that I stayed a Lexus customer. His name was Rocco. I also learned a ton from Rocco. I applied Rocco's customer service to my dental practice. I would arrange a ride for a patient who couldn't drive. If someone was having work done and they were from out of town, I would have a car meet them at the airport with drinks and snacks and bring them to the office. I tried to emulate Rocco's five-star service. Perhaps Rocco had a big part in the success of my business. So don't tell me that you can't change someone's life. Rocco changed mine.

Rocco retired several years ago and moved to Italy. His daughter took over his customers at the dealership. Before Rocco left, he called to tell me he was moving. He must have had hundreds of customers, but he made me feel as if I was special. I'm sure he did the same for all the others as well. He told me his daughter would take good care of me. I told him goodbye and extended my love and gratitude for his amazing service over the years. I hope he felt good after getting off the phone with me. He deserved at least that.

The time came when my car lease was up and I called his daughter. She was great and all, but she was no Rocco. She told me to come in to see the new cars. She did not offer to bring a car out to me. So I went in. I had trouble finding the dealership because they had moved and like I mentioned, I had never been there before.

I decided to lease a new RX Hybrid because of the new bells and whistles. The rest of the transaction was typical. When the car needed to be serviced, I had to make an appointment and a runner would bring out a loaner and leave the keys at the front desk of my office. The personal touch from Rocco was missing. It just wasn't the same.

So this year the lease on that car was up. I called about the lease, and Rocco's daughter told me to come in and look at the new cars. I had very few miles on mine because I live so close to work and don't take the car on trips. Because it was in such good shape, the buyout for my three-year-old car was expensive; in fact, it equalled the cost for me to get a brand new Toyota.

The Toyota RAV4 looks like the RX and drives like the RX and for all intents and purposes is the RX. Sure, it may not have the fancy wood-grained panels on the dash, but I was never that kind of guy anyway. I went online and compared new cars from all dealers and ended up deciding that before I would get a new Lexus, I would look at the RAV4 Hybrid (still wanted to be as green as I could).

It was the typical car dealership with the vultures ready to pounce when you got out of your car. Fortunately I had a name from correspondence online. So they let me pass the gauntlet of sales reps. And the lady was terrific. I have a friend, Joey, who owns a Toyota dealership in another state, and he told me to go in and meet the owner of this dealership and tell him that I was his friend. The guy was great. I felt like I was back with Rocco in some ways. We spent a lot of time in that dealership and the owner made me feel special.

Because I lost Rocco's personal service, we ended up getting the Toyota. There is no doubt that the service still would not be as good as Lexus's, even without Rocco. But with online car registration and the few times I would have to take the car in to be serviced, I didn't think it would be a big deal, certainly not worth the difference in price.

I have to tell you, though, I felt like I was cheating on Lexus. If I was Catholic, I would have gone to confession. I actually felt guilty. I know that if Rocco was still my sales rep I probably would be driving a Lexus today. No, I know I would. I was uncomfortable telling his daughter that I decided to get a Toyota. But she said, "As long as you're happy, I'm happy." And I am. I love my new car and the fact that I saved thousands of dollars for basically the same thing. Who knows, maybe I'll get another Lexus someday.

What's the real point of that story? With any business transaction or encounter, it's important for it to be a win-win for both you and the customer. My relationship with Rocco was a win-win. I got amazing service and a great car. Rocco got my business for the rest of his career. Short-term gain doesn't usually result in long-term gain unless it's a win-win. Rocco got a long-term gain because of his amazing service. We both benefited.

So what about you and your business? Is the customer benefiting? Are you benefiting? If you don't feel that you were adequately rewarded for your service, then you didn't win. If the customer feels it wasn't worth the cost, they didn't win.

Your Product Is Customer Service— No Matter What You Sell

In my opinion, Starbucks isn't successful because of the coffee; it's successful because of the service. Every store is the same; they have the same funky music, the same happy employees. Most every business is in the service business, not a product business. Yes, you may have a product that you offer for sale, but you really sell the service. It's all about perceived value. Is it a memorable event when customers or clients come in your business or buy something from you? If not, how can the experience be improved?

Ask yourself if your business can do better. If you offer an experience like Rocco, what effect will that have on your business. If you like the way you're treated in a particular store or shop or restaurant, ask yourself if that can possibly be done in your line of work.

In business there are usually two ways to succeed: quantity or quality. Many companies have become successful by providing products to the masses for a minimal profit. Overhead is usually higher, but the profit is created by the volume. Kmart might be an example of this. Quality, on the other hand, caters to a more selective crowd but has a higher-quality product with a better margin on each product. Nordstrom's might be the comparison to my Kmart example. Either can be successful but you need to choose wisely. It's interesting that Kmart filed for bankruptcy after the last recession.

Now, depending on your business, I would choose the quality over quantity. You can develop an identity, and you can develop a niche market based on your passion-driven purpose. You don't have to be all things to all people. If this is your passion-driven purpose, you also need to do it where you will be the happiest. Fulfilling your passion in a place where you are miserable does not lead to happiness.

The Fred Factor

In the book *The Fred Factor*, Fred is a mail carrier who goes that extra mile. Fred saw an opportunity to make a difference in the lives of those he served. He is an example of how passionate work can turn ordinary into extraordinary. Treat your customers as you would want to be treated. That's how you should look at everyone who comes into your business. If you were the customer, what would you want?

Another book that has valuable information about great service is *Delivering Knock Your Socks Off Service*. When I had my dental practice, we would have weekly team meetings. We would talk about important items, watch videos about techniques or procedures, and discuss ideas. I asked my team to read a chapter of this book before each meeting. I also prepared a three-question homework assignment. For example, "Do you think we could apply this to our office?" or "How can we take this idea and make it work in our office?" Just simple questions like that. These questions helped my team to understand the value of service and encouraged them think like an owner.

Customer service is critical to be successful in your passion-driven purpose. But the most important thing in life is happiness—the subject of our final step.

SUMMARY

- We are all in the service business.
- People's opinions of you are based on perception.
- Are you really doing the best you can?
- It's the customer who pays the wages.

Step Ten

Find Happiness—The Ultimate Success

Enjoying life is the ultimate success. Going from good to great requires happiness and enjoying what you do.

> Happiness is the only good.
> The time to be happy is now.
> The place to be happy is here.
> The way to be happy is to make others so.
> **—ROBERT GREEN INGERSOLL,**
> Civil War veteran, politician, and orator

What is the ultimate reason you should pursue your passion-driven purpose? Because if what you're doing is not your passion-driven purpose, you usually won't find the way to successful happiness. It's hard to be good at something you don't like doing. You won't practice, or spend downtime on it, or think about it afterhours.

> There may be peace without joy, and joy without peace,
> but the two combined make happiness.
> **—JOHN BUCHAN,** former governor general of Canada

If I hated golf, I wouldn't go to the driving range to practice. I wouldn't have bought a golf simulator. Why would I if I hated the game? The most successful athletes usually love their game. Michael Jordan would be at the gym shooting baskets before anyone else. It was the same with Kobe Bryant. They loved the game and wanted to spend all the time they could working on it.

Sadly, most people in my profession don't like being a dentist. It certainly isn't their passion-driven purpose. Very few take continuing education courses beyond their license requirements. Why would they spend time on something they don't like doing? Truth is, if they took more courses, they might find their passion within dentistry, like I did.

> A person often meets his destiny
> on the road he took to avoid it.
> **—JEAN DE LA FONTAINE,** French poet

Are you passionate about what you do? If not, can you find that passion doing what you do? Do you think you are excellent at what you do? Be honest! Even if you think you're good, there is an old saying that being good enough seldom is.

Are you also ethical in your pursuit of your goals? This is really important for your happiness. Are you not doing something right because it would be more expensive, or harder for you to do it right? Are you not correcting mistakes or wrong things because it'll cost you more to make it right for your customers? I've had dentists take shortcuts or do things haphazardly because they were in a hurry or they thought it wouldn't matter, but it came back to bite them. It takes a lot less time to do it right than it does to do something over.

Not doing the right thing the right way is unethical and then at the end of the day you have to be at peace with your decisions in your life. Are you? You need to self-reflect every once in a while. Ask yourself if you are doing the right thing? You could be the most successful person in your community, you could be the greatest at what you do in your community, but late at night when your eyes are closed and in the darkness of your bed, knowing you are not a good person, you're not going to be happy. You know in your heart what is right and what is wrong. Follow your heart.

> There is no right way to do the wrong thing.
> **—UNKNOWN**

There may be many things that you don't like about what you're doing that are making you unhappy. If so fix them! It could be one thing that you feel you have to do as part of your work, a procedure you do or a product you sell. If that's the case, then don't do it. What would happen if you stopped doing it? What effect would that have on your business? If it's someone who works for you and you're the boss, then fire them. What effect would that have on your business? If it's a co-worker, avoid them or see if you can be transferred. How much of an effect would it really have on your business or life? And let's say that it does, would it be worth it for happiness? It may be worth the sacrifice. If it is your boss, find a new job. I know it simplifies everything, but change is capable of happening in anyone's hands, and happiness is more important than any job.

> You cannot prevent the birds of sorrow
> from flying over your head, but you can prevent them
> from building nests in your hair.
> **—CHINESE PROVERB**

During my years in private practice, I sometimes worked with a difficult person who also seemed indispensable. But if that person left the practice, I usually saw no negative outcomes. In fact, most of the time the other team members were happy that person left. Every time that occurred, the work environment got better. Office morale improved.

At LVI, people often thought that the departure of a certain team member would be catastrophic to LVI. Not once, not one single time, did the dismissal or resignation of someone hurt LVI. It never hurt LVI because LVI was my passion-driven purpose, not theirs. Every time it happened, the departure helped my business. I don't regret one of those events. Each time the environment became a more successful, peaceful, happier place. And probably more importantly, the clients at our company were generally happy about the change.

Ego is out of control in my industry. It's probably true in yours as well. In dentistry, it has to do with a low self-esteem and ego is a way of compensating for that insecurity. What I've experienced is that ego is generally a defensive mechanism for a low self-esteem.

It was also not uncommon that when someone left the company, a lot of clients and employees would come out of the woodwork to tell me how much they hated that person. They wouldn't say anything to me because they thought I would be on his side. And once again, profits went up and team morale improved. If you're thinking it, why do you think the rest of the team is not thinking it? There is no such thing as an indispensable person.

Your Ideal World

If you had a magic wand and you could create your ideal world, what would make you the happiest? Take a few minutes, put the book down, and think about it. What would you like your world to be like? Where would you like to live?

> Life is the continuous adjustment of internal relations
> to external relations.
> **—HERBERT SPENCER,** English philosopher

Once you have come up with your ultimate life, ask yourself if that can that be accomplished? (Don't let your paradigms limit you.) If so, when can it be accomplished? Then go back to step 2 and set out a game plan to make that happen. I'm serious. Go through those steps to create your plan to achieve this dream. There is nothing more important in life than to be happy.

You know the old saying that money can't buy happiness. It can't. I also know the saying of W.C. Fields, "Money will not buy happiness, but it will let you be unhappy in nice places." There is nothing wrong with wanting and having money. It's a good thing but it won't make you really happy. I told you about the happiness index earlier in this book to prove it. Happiness was not dependent on someone's wealth or lack of wealth.

> Happiness doesn't depend on what we have
> but it depends on how we feel toward what we have.
> We can be happy with little and miserable with much.
> **—WILLIAM DEMPSTER HOARD,** American politician

I'm going to bare my soul to you now. I've had an amazing life. I've lived the dream. But it hasn't been all roses and champagne. There have been many events in my life in which I was at the bottom of the pit, and others where I was at the top of the peak. It's interesting that I love roller coasters because that's been my life. From traumatic events, to gut wrenching incidences, to relationship dissolutions, to dysfunctional family matters— it's been quite a ride. I'm at peace with everything now. I've eliminated a lot of negativity from my life. I'm with my soul mate and will be for the rest of my life. I'm a happy man.

I haven't always been well off. In dental school I was poor and on food stamps and living in a small apartment. After dental school I was in a residency program making a meagre living but very happy to be out of school and starting my adult chapter of my life. For the first ten years of my private practice, I was not an overly successful dentist. At the end of those first ten years I hated being a dentist. As I mentioned before, if I could have done anything else, I would have. Although I was making progress, I had no passion-driven purpose.

I made changes to my life because of two men. Dr. Cal Evans, who at the time was maybe the most successful dentist in town and a friend who became a mentor to me. He gave me lots of advice that helped me in my practice. But the best thing he did for me was to convince me to go to a weekend seminar by Dr. Omer Reed. Omer changed my life by giving me the passion-driven purpose I needed. Love and gratitude, Cal and Omer!

I didn't have to find my passion; it was there all along. I had let "things" get in the way—the management hassles, the frustrations, the lack of gratitude from clients, as well as the daily mundane things I was experiencing. After that weekend I realized that I needed to concentrate on the passion of creating a business that was based around helping people by making them happy and maybe even changing their lives.

> You're a happy fellow, for you'll give happiness and joy to many other people. There is nothing better or greater than that!
> **—LUDWIG VAN BEETHOVEN,** German composer and pianist

I have spent the rest of my life devoted to that passion-driven purpose. LVI is the by-product of that dedication to my passion-driven purpose, and every advancement, business opportunity, and evolutionary change is also a by-product of my plan to achieve it.

So what's my point of telling you all this? I've been poor when I was young and naive, but I was happy. Maybe it's true that ignorance is bliss. I thought I had so much when I graduated from dental school, making $18,000 a year in a residency program. Relatively speaking, I did have a lot, because I was poor before that. I thought I was in heaven. One of the first things I did was to buy a motorcycle. I would drive that motorcycle to the airport to take flying lessons. And in no time, I was a private pilot. As a sort of Renaissance man, I wanted to do everything. I also learned to scuba dive. I was poor, but I was happy.

I've also been rich and unhappy. My newfound passion became making people happy and changing their lives through cosmetic dentistry.

That field was in its infancy and no dental school taught it. As I mentioned in the introduction, I was asked to lecture by a local lab on tooth-colored restorations. As it turns out, I had a natural gift for that. Soon I was traveling 120 days a year while maintaining a successful private practice. I was asked in 1993 to be part of the first live patient postgraduate educational program at Baylor College of Dentistry in Dallas.

In my effort to stay home more to be with my first son, Dylan, I came up with an idea of doing these programs in Las Vegas, where I was born and raised and was living. So LVI was started at my private dental practice as I lectured while sitting on the counter of our lunchroom. The small team lounge was packed. As we outgrew the space, I had to rent rooms for the lectures at the YMCA next door. Eventually I built the first building on the current LVI campus, a 20,000-square-foot building with a large entry rotunda, ten operatories, two lecture halls, a small lunch room, a hands-on laboratory, business office upstairs, and a private practice facility.

People said I was crazy. Many wanted me to fail out of jealousy and some did all they could to make that happen. I owe a lot to those jealous people because they made me work even harder to make my venture succeed. I would sleep maybe four hours a night and spend hours on the road, lecturing and working on my projects for LVI.

I remained a committed father. I would read my sons a story every night when I put them to bed. They wouldn't want me to leave, so I would sit in the hall in between each of their rooms, working on my computer where they could hear me until they fell asleep. They would think I was gone and would yell, "Dad?" and I would say, "I'm still here, still here!" I would then take a red-eye flight, taking Nyquil so I could sleep on the plane, arrive the next morning and lecture. I would then get on a plane at the end of the lecture to fly home so I could be with them that evening and put them to bed. It was good that most of the time I was going East to West because the time zone change made that possible.

I had everything going for me. I was a famous dentist in high demand, making good money, and had the president of a major dental company call me the most influential dentist in America. I'm not sure if that's true, but I know I was affecting the lives of lots of dentists and their patients. Yep, I had everything going for me except one thing: a happy marriage.

LVI had become my mistress. It was the only passion in my life because I had none at home. I was rich, but I wasn't happy. I had resigned to the belief that marriage was like that. My friends' marriages reinforced that belief. I knew something was missing in me and my life, and I was trying to fill it with my passion-driven purpose, my work. Who knows, maybe my business wouldn't be where it is today had I not had this emptiness inside me.

My attitude about all this was my choice. I chose to be positive to everybody around me. I portrayed a happy man, full of jokes and funny stories. But it wasn't true. I was very unhappy inside. I made the decision to be happy to the world and was happy when engaged in my passion-driven purpose.

> "He alone is the happy man who has learned
> to extract happiness not from ideal conditions
> but from actual ones about him."
> **—ANONYMOUS**

So there you have it. I've been poor and happy, and I've been rich and unhappy. I would choose poor and happy over rich and unhappy every time. If somebody gave you an ultimatum right now and said you could either be poor and happy or rich and unhappy, what would you choose? In a heartbeat, I would be poor and happy.

The good news is now I'm rich and happy. It's definitely the best of the three! The void in my life has been filled, which provides the inner peace and happiness that is so important. I'm married to my best friend and the love of my life. We are not only life partners, but business partners as well. LVI would not be where it is today if it were not for her. I don't even think LVI would still be here if it wasn't for her. I know I probably wouldn't be involved.

She made the trials and tribulations all these years manageable. She has made it succeed in a way that allows me to focus on the "mission." She's not only a very talented dentist, she has many other talents that make the company flow like well-oiled machine. She's made work fun for me, and we are able to share and understand what and why we feel the way we do about work. So many have told me I'm a better person since Heidi entered my life. Together with our close friends and our immediate family, we are living the dream. Remember Bessie Anderson Stanely's definition of success at the beginning of this book? I've achieved success!

> He has achieved success who has lived well, laughed often,
> and loved much who . . . has never lacked appreciation of
> Earth's beauty . . . who has always looked for the best in others.
> **—BESSIE ANDERSON STANLEY,** American writer

I worry that my story may make some of you jealous and critical, and maybe even angry. If you feel that, please reread step 4. There is no advancement toward your dreams if you are spending energy being jealous of mine.

There is also no reason that you can't start each day smiling. It's your choice. Do you enjoy your family? More importantly, do they enjoy you? Do you appreciate your friends, or do you discard them when they can no longer help you? Do you use people and take advantage of them, or are you loyal to those who helped you become who you are? Do you express love and gratitude? Do you have lasting friendships?

> When you arise in the morning, think of what a precious privilege
> it is to be alive, to breathe, to think, to enjoy, to love.
> **—MARCUS AURELIUS,** Roman emperor

Heidi gave me this quote when she first met me because it reminded her of me.

> A master in the art of living draws no sharp distinction between his work and his play, his labour and his leisure, his mind his body, his education and his recreation. He hardly knows which is which, he simply pursues his vision of excellence through whatever he is doing and leaves others to determine whether he is working or playing. To himself he always appears to be doing both.
> **—FRANCOISE RENE AUGUSTE CHATEAUBRIAND,**
> French writer, politician, diplomat and historian

Let's end this book with these questions: Are you enjoying life? Can you be silly and have fun? Will you let your kids paint your face? Will you wear silly outfits for a party? Do you never say you're too old to do something? As my son called me, are you just a "big kid"? Can you find that inner kid in you and let it come out again? Can you choose to be happy?

In *The Traveler's Gift*, the author offers decisions that determine personal success: accept responsibility, seek wisdom, be a person of action, have a committed heart, have a forgiving spirit, persist without exception, and choose to be happy. Remember, it's your choice.

So there you are, the ten steps up the ladder to success.

1. *Find your passion-driven purpose.*

2. *Create your vision.* Make a business plan to achieve your dream.

3. *Attitude.* It's the one thing in life you have complete control over.

4. *Eliminate jealousy.* It's a destructive trait that will make you unhappy.

5. *Control irrational fears that prevent success.* Have courage to take action!

6. *Create the desire and the drive to succeed.* You must want it badly.

7. *Persevere.* Don't give up. You may be closer than you think.

8. *Be teachable.* It's absolutely necessary to achieve success.

9. *Serve others.* The customer is your boss.

10. *Achieve happiness.* Success is meaningless without it—the ultimate success.

How do those ten steps affect your talent?

1. A passionate purpose energizes your talents and makes life worth it.

2. Belief in your vision lifts your talents, and teamwork multiplies your talents.

3. Attitude creates positive results.

4. Eliminating jealousy focuses you on *your* talents, not those of others.

5. Courage expands your talents with no limits or restrictions.

6. Desire activates your talents and puts them into action.

7. Perseverance sustains your talents.

8. Teachability sharpens your talents and feeds the passion.

9. Service shares your talents with others, which is what it's all about.

10. Happiness and enjoying life rewards your talents, the ultimate success.

I want to sincerely thank you for giving me this opportunity to, in some small way, touch your lives; and in a big way for reading this book. Thank you for letting me live my dream and hopefully helping you live yours.

Love and Gratitude to All of You,

Resources

Books that contributed to the content of this book as research over the years:

Leadership: The Inner Side of Greatness by Peter Koestenbaum

Talent Is Never Enough by John C. Maxwell

Good to Great by Jim Collins

Our Iceberg Is Melting by John Kotter

Becoming a Category of One by Joe Calloway

It's Not What Happens to You, It's What You Do About It by W. Mitchell

Waiting For Your Cat to Bark by Bryan and Jeffrey Eisenberg

The Traveller's Gift by Andy Andrews

The Precious Present by Spencer Johnson

Think and Grow Rich by Napoleon Hill

The Richest Man in Babylon by George S. Clason

The Last Tycoon by F. Scott Fitzgerald

Marketing to Win by Frank K. Sonneberg

Primal Leadership by Daniel Goleman

The Fred Factor by Mark Sanborn

Power of Impossible Thinking by Norman Vincent Peale

Naked Conversations by Robert Scoble and Shel Israel

The Seven Spiritual Laws of Success by Deepak Chopra

The Simple Truths of Service by Ken Blanchard

The Tipping Point by Malcolm Gladwell

The Dip by Seth Godin

The Ten Faces of Innovation by Tom Kelley/Jonathan Littman

The 8th Habit by Stephen R. Covey

Business @ The Speed of Thought by Bill Gates

Delivering Knock Your Socks Off Service by Kristin Anderson and Ron Zemke

The Pursuit of WOW by Tom Peters

Who Moved My Cheese by Spencer Johnson

The Hidden Messages in Water by Masuru Emoto

Who's Life Are You Living? Discovering the Wisdom to Walk in Freedom by Chidi Jacob

ABOUT THE AUTHOR

D r. Dickerson was born and raised in Las Vegas, Nevada. He attended public school, went to the University of the Pacific for undergraduate training in Stockton, California, and then went to the University of the Pacific School of Dentistry in San Francisco. Upon graduation at the age of twenty-three, he completed a residency program in Fresno, California.

After his residency program, Dr. Dickerson was busy creating a practice; however, he was increasingly frustrated and disenchanted by the traditional approach to dental care and the lack of business training in dental school and in post graduate courses. Developing a "Patient-Centered Practice" gave him his passion-driven purpose. Propelled by this new excitement for dentistry, Dr. Dickerson started sharing his passion with other dentists and quickly became recognized as a respected opinion leader and highly sought-after speaker, as well as one of the most influential people in dentistry. He wrote two books on this philosophy, *The Exceptional Dental Practice* and its sequel, *In Search of the Ultimate Practice*. He was instrumental as a pioneer in the aesthetic revolution in dentistry and later in igniting and advancing physiologically based dentistry. His focus for the past three decades has been to create a better future for the profession, and to provide better service and care for the public.

In 1993, Dr. Dickerson was asked by Baylor College of Dentistry to develop their first postgraduate live patient treatment program. Since 1994, in an effort to be home more with his first son, Dr. Dickerson's efforts were channeled into creating the Las Vegas Institute for Advanced Dental Studies (LVI Global), providing an educational forum for advancing the profession. The construction of the existing campus was opened in 1998 and was expanded to 63,000 square feet of buildings on five acres in 2003 in the beautiful Summerlin area of Las Vegas to create an environment that enhances the learning experience of the attendees. For the past twenty-three years, LVI has led the way in continuing education and has become the world's premier postgraduate educational center in dentistry.

Thousands of dentists from all over the world have attended LVI, and thousands of their patients have been treated there, as well as the thousands of others who have enhanced their practices by attending lectures by Dr. Dickerson. His books also help dentists achieve their dreams. He also wrote, *How To Create an Exceptional Aesthetic Practice: Ten Dentists That Have Done It* and *Unleashing the Power of Dentistry.* Dr. Dickerson has also published hundreds of articles and lectured in every state and most Western countries.

From aesthetic dentistry to scientifically based occlusal approaches, Bill has encouraged, assisted, motivated and propelled dentists and their teams from over forty-three nations to grow and excel. He has developed many aesthetic and occlusal techniques, products, and procedures that enhance comprehensive restorative procedures that improve the lives of thousands of patients. He has received numerous professional awards and honors while becoming one of the most accomplished people in his profession.

While working on his passion-driven purpose, he has been dedicated to his family by balancing his personal and professional life. This includes coaching his children in sports, being part of their everyday lives, and adjusting his business schedule around theirs. In addition to his work and family, he enjoys flying, golf, roller coasters, and pure adrenaline adventures.

Made in the USA
Monee, IL
18 February 2021

60836615R00087